Anonymus

Handbook of Dr. Kahn's Museum

Anonymus

Handbook of Dr. Kahn's Museum

ISBN/EAN: 9783741144875

Manufactured in Europe, USA, Canada, Australia, Japa

Cover: Foto ©Thomas Meinert / pixelio.de

Manufactured and distributed by brebook publishing software
(www.brebook.com)

Anonymus

Handbook of Dr. Kahn's Museum

HANDBOOK

OF

DR. KAHN'S

MUSEUM

3, TICHBORNE STREET,

FACING THE HAYMARKET

London:

PRINTED BY J. SEALE, HAYLES STREET, SOUTHWARK.

———

1867

INTRODUCTION.

THE following magnificent collection, which has been brought to its present state by the labour and study of nearly Twenty years, and at an expenditure of more than Ten Thousand Pounds, is designed to afford to the Public an opportunity of acquainting themselves how they " LIVE, AND MOVE, AND HAVE THEIR BEING."

Under these three comprehensive heads, which the genius of the poet has strung tersely together in one line, are comprised all the phenomena included in the sciences of anatomy and physiology.

Although this knowledge is, beyond question, of the utmost importance to all, there are few who possess even a smattering of such information, more especially as regards the last point how we " have our being." A false sense of propriety has not only prevented the discussion of this subject, but rendered it most difficult to obtain reliable information even on the part of those who diligently seek it.

The *Lancet, Medical Times,* and the whole of the general as well as Medical press have attested in the strongest terms, the high value and utility of this collection.

CATALOGUE, &c.

The Wonderful Developement of the Human Fœtus.
The preparations are real, and are preserved
in spirits. They show the developement of the
child from about ten days after conception to
forty weeks. In some of the earlier preparations
a portion of the womb has been removed; and
in others a delicate membrane may be seen surrounding the embryo. This membrane is called
the *amnion*, and contains fluid, so as to protect
the child from the contraction of the womb.
This fluid it is which escapes on the rupture of
the membranes at the birth of the child. It is
called, in scientific language, the *liquor amnii.*

1 An embryo 10 days old.	18 A fœtus 17 weeks old.
2 do. 12 do.	19 do. 18 do.
3 do. 2 wks. old.	20 do. 19 do.
4 do. 3 do.	21 do. 20 do.
5 do. 4 do.	22 do. 21 do.
6 do. 5 do.	23 do. 22 do.
7 A fœtus 6 do.	24 do. 23 do.
8 do. 7 do.	25 do. 24 do.
9 do. 8 do.	26 do. 25 do.
10 do. 9 do.	27 do. 26 do.
11 do. 10 do.	28 do. 27 do.
12 do. 11 do.	29 do. 28 do.
13 do. 12 do.	30 do. 29 do.
14 do. 13 do.	31 do. 30 do.
15 do. 14 do.	32 do. 31 do.
16 do. 15 do.	33 do. 32 do.
17 do. 16 do.	34 do. 33 do.

35 A fœtus 24 weeks old, laid open and the liver
   injected.
36 A negro fœtus 25 weeks old.
37 A fœtus 36 weeks old.
38   do.   37   do.   born without brain.
39 · do.   38   do.
40   do.   39   do.
41   do.   40   do.   in its natural position in the
       womb.

42 A fœtus with two bodies, but only one.head
   (real).
43 Twins in the 16th week of pregnancy. One
   is still enveloped in its encompassing
   membrane, but the other is deprived of it.
44 The heart of a newly-born child, laid open.
45 Sexual organs of a young female in a state
   of virginity, showing the hymen.
46 Natural uterus, with its appendages.
47 An adult's brain, weighing 3lbs., attached
   to which are seen the eyes, appended to
   the optic nerves.
48 The tongue, larynx, windpipe, lungs, and
   heart, of a newly-born child.
49 A testicle and epididymus injected with
   mercury.
50 A petrified uterus in the third month of
   pregnancy.
51 A heart injected; the arteries red and the
   veins blue.
52 The right side of the heart; the chambers
   and veins injected.
53 The left side of the heart; the chambers
   and arteries injected.

54	Articulated skeleton of a fœtus, 2 months old.

55	do.	do.	3	do.
56	do.	do.	4	do.
57	do.	do.	5	do.
57*	do.	do.	22 weeks old.
57+	do.	do.	23	do.
58	do.	do.	6 months old.
59	do.	do.	7	do.
60	do.	do.	8	do.
61	do.	do.	9	do.

62 Glass case, containing the skeleton of a fœtus, 9 months old, which is taken entirely to pieces, so that each bone can be examined separately.

63 Male skeleton, with moveable articulations

64 Female skeleton, with moveable articulations

65 Cranium of a fœtus 7 months old.

66 Cranium of a fœtus 9 months old.

66a Enlargement of the head, the result of hydrocephalus, or water on the brain.

67 Cranium of a monkey (simia capucina).

68 Cranium of an ourang outang.

69 A human cranium—one side of which is divided according to Dr. Spurzheim's system of phrenology, and the other according to that of Dr. Gall.

70 Female pelvis, well formed.

71 do. deformed.

72 Upper portion of a skull showing the mode in which the operation of trephining is performed.

73 Internal ear, showing the lining membrane and the auricular bones.

74 Natural preparation, showing the first and second sets of teeth. The milk-teeth have, for the most part, made their appearance through the alveoli; while the second, or permanent set, may be seen imbedded in the jaw, and gradually advancing to the surface.

75 A fœtus, 9 months old, born at Ghent, with two heads (real).

76 A stone found in the spleen of a girl, 11 years old.

77 Ditto found in the gall-bladder of a boy, 15 years old.

78 Ditto found in the bladder of a female, 24 years old.

80 A tape-worm, 50 yards long, passed by a female child eight years of age. These parasitic animals are frequently caused by permitting children to use large quantities of sugar; their eggs having been frequently discovered, not only in that substance, but also in some of the inferior kinds of flour. A child, suffering from these tormenting pests gradually wastes away, and relief can only be obtained by their expulsion.

81 A tape-worm, 80 yards long, extracted from the body of a boy seven years old.

82 A heart affected with hypertrophy.

Muscles, Veins, Arteries, and Nerves.

The models in the ensuing series are made

from leather, by a patent process, and were placed
in a prominent position in the Great Exhibition
of 1851, where they met with the most unequi-
vocal testimonies of approbation from the leading anatomists of England and the Continent.
They are intended to show the distribution of
the muscles, arteries, veins and nerves, which
they do with the utmost fidelity to nature.   The
arteries are coloured *red*, the veins *blue*, and the
nerves *white*;   and it will be observed that
wherever a large number of vessels are congre-
gated they are invariably placed in a secluded
position, the arteries being always subjacent to
the veins, so as to avoid the serious effects which
would accrue from their injury.

The exquisite beauty of these preparations
cannot fail to strike the most superficial observer.

83 Head with the skin taken off on the right
side, so that the arteries, veins, and
nerves may be seen.

84 The arm elevated with the hollow of the
armpit injected.

85 An arm which exhibits the superficial veins
of the external surface injected.

86 Ditto of the internal surface.

87 An arm, on the internal surface of which the
more deeply-seated blood vessels and
nerves are shown in their natural condition.

88 The calf of the right leg, showing the blood
vessels and nerves situated on its internal
surface.

89 The external surface of the same.

90 The ham of the leg, showing the arteries, veins, and nerves situated in this region.

91 All the superior parts of the groin and thigh, with the blood-vessels injected.

92 The abdominal region, where the parts most exposed to rupture are exactly copied from nature.

93 Perpendicular section of the male pelvis, showing *a*, the right kidney; *b*, ureter; *c*, bladder; *d*, the seminal vesicles; *e*, urethra; *f*, the penis cut perpendicularly.

94 Male pelvis, exhibiting, besides all the parts indicated in the preceding, the vessels that convey the semen from the testes into the seminal vesicles.

95 Female pelvis, cut perpendicularly, in which are seen the following parts:—viz., *a*, the urinary bladder; *b*, the urinary passage; *c*, the vagina; *d*, the womb; *e*, the ovary; and *f*, the rectum.

96 A less central section of the same parts, showing the arteries and veins situated in that region.

97 A verticle section of the female pelvis showing the following parts:—*a*, os pubis; *b*, bladder; *c*, urinary passage; *d*, vagina; *e*, mouth of the womb; *f*, the womb, containing *g*, a fœtus three months old; and *h*, the rectum.

100 A head with the skin of the right side taken off, in which are exhibited the most minute, superficial veins of the face; the parotid gland, with its duct;

the right pupil opens, and the eye is divided vertically.

101 A head, vertically cut, showing—a, hair of the brain; b, cerebellum; c, the prolonged medullary body; spinal marrow; e, nasal septum; f, buccal cavity; g, os-hyodies; h, tongue; and i, windpipe.

102 Part of the skull, showing the deep vein of the face in their relation with the arteries.

103 A part of the cranium, representing the distribution of the first seven pairs of the cerebra nerves, and a portion of the great sympathetic.

104 An adult's brain in wax, which can be taken entirely to pieces.

105 Wax model of the head of a female idiot, named Sukey Hillings. She was a native of Suffolk, and was 5 feet 3 inches in height. She died at the age of 60.

106 Wax model of a idiot, who died at Amsterdam. The bust was taken by Dr. Spurzheim, in the year 1820, at which time the idiot was 25 years of age.

107 Model of the head of an ourang-outang.

109 This represents the first process of deglutition, in which the food is seen between the incisor teeth.

110 It is now between the molar teeth or grinders

111 The food is here seen at the entrance of the pharynx.

112 The food is now entirely in the œsophagus.

113 Preparation showing all the muscles by which the process of deglutition is carried on.

———————

120 A life size model, showing all the superficial muscles in the human body.

120*a* A miniature model of a similar character.

121 East Indian girl, 12 years old, playing with a parrot. The bird is held in one hand, and some cherries in the other—the expression of the countenance being radiant with childish delight. The spine is laid open throughout its course, showing the connection established by its means between the brain and the lower extremities.

122 Girl, seven years old, exhibiting the dorsal spine opened, to show the spinal marrow, with the nerves which issue therefrom.

123 THE APOLLO BELVIDERE.—This magnificent figure is of the male sex, full size, and takes entirely to pieces. It may be considered the *chef-d'œuvre* of anatomical science ; and the highest enconiums have been passed upon it by the medical and general press. The whole of the structure of the human body is here exposed to view, enabling the spectator to contemplate the mechanism by which the vital actions are carried on, the delicacy of the different organs, and the beautiful provisions made against their injury, or, for their reparation in case of accident. The figure is re-

11

clining on a couch of crimson velvet, and on the skin being removed from the body, arms, leg, and face all the superficial and deep-seated muscles, arteries, veins and nerves, situate on those parts are exposed. These in turn remove, showing the cavities of the body. The human body is divided into two large cavities; 1st, the cranium, containing the organs by which the mental powers are manifested; and 2nd, the trunk, containing the organs which serve principally to minister to the corporeal wants. The latter is again subdivided into two: the thorax, occupied by the lungs, heart, &c., and the abdomen, occupied by the stomach, liver, intestines, kidneys, and other smaller and more unimportant organs.

124 THE VENUS MEDICIS.—This figure may be considered one of the most beautiful in the museum. By it every portion of the female figure is presented to view. It resembles the Apollo, except in the fact that one is male, the other female.

125 Full-length female figure laid open, for the purpose of showing the internal conformation of the body in a perfectly healthy condition.—The letters denote as follows: a, right lobe of the lung; b, left lobe of the lung slightly thrown back; c, heart; d, pericardium, or covering of the heart, laid open and reflected; e, aorta, or arterial trunk; f, pleura, or covering of the .

lungs, laid open; *g*, ensiform and costal cartilages ; *h*, diaphragm, or midriff; *i*, liver; *j*, gall bladder; *k*, stomach; *l*, spleen ; *m*, small intestines ; *n*, part of the large intestines ; *o*, os pubis ; *p*, bladder ; *q*, uterus or womb, laid open, and containing a fœtus 2 months after conception, attached by means of the umbilical cord, to *r*, the placenta, or after-birth.

126 This figure is a most beautiful piece of artistic work, and has been recently completed at immense labor and cost. The abdomen is laid open, for the purpose of showing the position of the viscera when displaced by the uterus in the later months of gestation. The period represented is about 8 months, and it will be observed how enormously the womb is enlarged, and how, by its increase in size, it has changed the position of all the other organs situated in the abdominal cavity.

127 Full-length figure representing the natural position of the child at the time of birth.

128 Figure of Mercury, from the antique.
129 Ditto, Venus de Medicus.
137 A man's hand, with the ends of the fingers laid open, exhibiting the ramifications of the nerve which produces the sense of touch.
138 Cast from the hand of a gardener at Wazemmes, near Lisle, named Cordonnier.

139 A human tongue, magnified five times, showing the three sorts of papillœ, which communicate the sense of taste, viz:—*a*, the lenticular; *b*, the fungiform; *c*, the filiform.

140 Transverse section of the nose, showing the Schneiderian or pituitary membrane, and the nerves of smell, with their branches.

141 An ear, greatly magnified, which can be taken to pieces.

142 Natural cranium, in which the auricular organs are clearly seen.

143 Natural preparation, showing the four auricular bones, with the labyrinth and cochlea.

144 Section of the head. The bougie is introduced into the *eustachian tube* through the nose.

145 A magnified eye, which can be taken to pieces as follows;—the white tunic or sclerotic, the cornea, the iris with the pupil, the crystalline lens with its capsule, the vitreous humour, the optic nerve, and the muscles.

156 Full-length model of one of those interesting and curious specimens of humanity exhibited in this country a few years ago, called Bosjesmen, or Bushmen.

157 A woman of the same race.

A 3

158 A full-length portrait model of the little
Aztec boy, as he was called. These
curious beings created a great sensation
in this country a few years ago, and certainly it is difficult to conceive anything
more interesting. That the tale told of
their capture is true, no man of sense
probably believes; that they were the
descendants of so fine a race of people as
the old Aztecs, is more than questionble ;
but that they were most remarkable
beings, no one will deny.

159 The Aztec girl, so called.

175 Head of a New Zealand Chief (real)

————

*The following collection of Models serve to illus-
trate some important facts in Histology, or
Microscopic Anatomy.*

203 A vertical section of the skin, from the in-
side of the thumb, magnified 20 times.

204 The same on a smaller scale.

205 Compound papillæ of the palm of the hand,
magnified 60 times.

206 Horizontal section of the skin from the heel
of the foot.

207 Two single papillæ from the palm of the
hand, magnified 350 times.

208 Bundles of muscular fibres, anastomising
with each other, magnified 20 times.

209 Portion of one of the bundles of muscular
fibres, magnified 350 times.

210 Fat cells from the mammary gland of the
female, magnified 350 times.

211 The same fat cells, having been treated
    with ether.
212 Fat cells, with margarin acid crystals.
213 A few forms of fat cells as they appear
    in dropsy, magnified 350 times.
214 Blood vessels of a fat cell magnified 100 times
215 Three fat cells, with capillary vessels,
    magnified 100 times.
216 Vessels of the papillæ of the skin.
217 Two papillæ from the palm of the hand,
    showing the origin of the nerves.
218 Four papillæ, treated with caustic potash,
    magnified 100 times.
219 Twofold division of a nerve from the plexus
    in the glans-penis.
220 Threefold division of the same.
221 Nerve of the bulb of the conjunctiva.
222 Small ganglion of the conjunctiva, entering
    in one branch and emerging in two.
223 Horizontal layer of the epidermis, from the
    back of the hand, magnified 50 times:
    showing the grooves for the reception
    of the papillæ.
224 Vertical section of the epidermis, and the
    external corium from the inside of the
    thumb, magnified 50 times.
225 Four scales of the epidermis, magnified
    350 times.
226 Five lamillæ from the epidermis, magnified
    250 times.
227 Scales of the epidermis, boiled in acetic acid,
    forming vesicles, magnified 350 times.
228 Same, boiled in caustic potash.

16

248 A hair-bulb, magnified 350 times.

249 A hair-bulb of the eyebrow, magnified 50
    times.

250 Origin of the papillæ pilli of the hair.

251 First development of the bulb of the hair,
    not yet through the skin.

252 The same, with the hair through the skin.

253 Hair-bulb from the chest of an embryo, 17
    weeks old—hair not yet through the skin.

254 Five views of the hair from the eyelash of
    a child 1 year old, magnified 20 times.

255 Sweat gland, with the arteries injected,
    magnified 35 times.

256 Canal of a sweat gland.

257 The same, curved.

258 The end of a large sweat gland, from the
    axilla, magnified 350 times.

259 Epidermis from the palm of the hand,
    viewed from the inside.

260 Commencement of sweat glands, from an
    embryo 5 months old, magnified 50 times.

261 Single sweat gland, magnified 350 times.

262 Commencement of sweat glands in the
    fœtus, 6 months old, magnified 50 times.

263 The same, from a fœtus, 7 months old.

264 A coil of a sweat gland, from a fœtus, 6
    months old.

265 Bulb sheath of a very strong hair, mag-
    nified 300 times.

266 Hair and hair sheath, middle size, magni-
    fied 50 times.

267 A portion of a grey-hair, the marrow filled
    with air.

18

268 Tho same, the air having been removed by
turpentine oil.

———

EMBRYOLOGY.

269 The female sexual organs laid open—*a*,
greater labia or lips; *b*, inner labia or
nymphæ; *c*, clitoris; *d*, vagina; *e*, urethra; *f*, womb; *g*, mouth of the womb;
h, left ovary; *i*, right ovary laid open;
j j, fallopian tubes; *k, k*, fringed or fim-
briated extremities of the fallopian tubes.
270 Spermatozoa 500 times magnified.
271 Spermatozoa 1000 times magnified.
272 An ovary, showing the Graafian vesicles.
273 The fallopian tube laid open, showing the
fecundated ovum.
274 Immature female ovum or egg, 300 times
magnified.
275 Mature female ovum, 300 times magnified.
275a Impregnated female ovum, 300 times magnified. By the three foregoing figures
it will be seen that the female egg in an
immature condition is composed of a con-
geries of cells, with a larger one in the
centre, which, as the egg advances towards maturity, rises to its surface, forming the germinal spot. On this becoming
impregnated by the attachment of the
spermatozoon, a small white stripe is
found on the germinal spot, and this
shape is termed the *nota primitiva*.

276 Section of the womb and ovary, showing
the mode in which the egg is seized by
the fringed extremity of the fallopian
tube—*a*, the womb ; *b*, passage for the
ovum ; *c*, mucous secretion in the womb,
or deciduary membrane ; *d*, fringed ends
of the fallopian tube ; *e*, ovary laid open ;
f, enlargement of the Graafian vesicle,
containing the ovum.

277 Ovary of a girl who had apparently never
copulated, but in whom, after death, a
yellow spot, formed by the departure of
the ovum, and called the corpus luteum,
was found in the ovary. This accords
with Dr. Bischoff's theory, who says that
ova sometimes detach themselves during
menstruation, or as the result of onanism.

278 An ovary taken from an old woman, who
it was supposed had never copulated, yet
in the ovary, several old copora lutea
are discoverable.

279 Ovary of a woman who died seven months
after conception, showing a recent corpus
luteum.

280 Ovary of a woman who died four weeks
after confinement, showing the corpus
luteum.

281 Representation of the mode in which the
Graafian vesicle bursts on the impregnation of the ovum. The fringed end of
the fallopian tube is seizing the ovary, and
the egg, passing into it, is carried along
the tube into the womb to be developed,

pushing back the deciduary membrane as
it enters—e, ovary laid open; f, the
Graulian vesicle burst; b, fallopian tube
laid open; at the extremity of which is
seen the ovum detached from the ovary,
and arriving in the womb.

282 The womb of a girl who died suffocated,
and who had, shortly before her death,
an ovum detached from the ovary, which
was found in the fallopian tube; in the
womb itself may be observed the mucous
secretion, called the deciduary membrane.

283 Womb, laid open, unimpregnated; therefore
the mucous secretion is not found.

*Formation and development of the first traces of a
Fœtus.*

284 A human embryo in the first days of its
fecundation—a, chorion, or enveloping
membrane.

285 A human embryo still more developed—a,
embryo; b, amnion c, vascular area; d,
blood vessels of the yelk of the embryo;
c, chorion.

286 A human embryo further developed—a,
embryo; b, amnion c, vascular area;
d, chorion.

287 A human embryo yet more advanced—a,
embryo; b, amnion; c, vascular area;
d, chorion; e, first appearance of the villi;
f, allantoid membrane.

288 A human embryo still more developed—*a*,
embryo ; *b*, amnion ; *c*, vascular area ; *d*,
blood-vessels of the chorion ; *e*, allantoid
membrane.

289 A human embryo further developed—*a*,
embryo ; *b*, vascular area ; *c*, allantoid
membrane , which is already attached to
the chorion so as to form the umbilical
or navel cord ; *d*, chorion ; *e*, villi ; *f*,
amnion.

———

*Representation of the more advanced development
of the Human Egg in the womb.*

290 Natural size of the human embryo about
the 3rd week of pregnancy.

291 A human embryo magnified in the 3rd
week of pregnancy, showing how the
vessels of the allantoid membrane extend ·
themselves through the chorion, thus
effecting the union between the mother
and the child—*a*, allantoid membrane,
changed into the umbilical cord ; *b*, amnion, in which the embryo is enclosed ;
c, the umbilical vesicle ; *d*, chorion divided ; *e*, villi ; *f*, point where the deciduary membrane is reflected; *g*, decidua
reflexa ; *h*, decidua vera ; *k*, chorion ; *m*,
mouth of the womb, closed by a mucous
deposit.

292 Magnified embryo in the 5th week of pregnancy—*a*, umbilical or navel cord ; *b*, am-

nion, in which the embryo is enclosed ;
c, umbilical vesicle ; d, umbilical cord ;
e, villi ; f, point where the deciduary
membrane is reflected ; g, inner decidua ;
h, outer decidua ; i, mucous secretion ; f,
mouth of the womb.

292a Human embryo aged about 14 days—the
embryo still partly receives its nourish-
ment from the yelk, from which it is
separated only by a short canal.

293 An embryo of 14 days magnified—a, the
hemispheres ; b, vesicle of the copora
quadrigemina, or middle lobes of the
brain ; c, cerebellum ; d, eyes ; e, parts of
the face which form the jaws ; f, heart ;
g, surface of the abdomen ; h, surface of
the loins ; i, umbilical cord ; j, umbilical
vesicle ; i, posteriors.

294 A human embryo 3 weeks old, natural size.

295 Magnified size of a human embryo 3 weeks
old—a, vesicle of the corpora quadrigemina ; b, hemispheres ; c, eyes ; d, cerebellum ; e, rudiments of the upper jaw ;
f, rudiments of the tongue ; g, rudiments
of the lower jaw and of the tongue bone ;
h, heart ; i, surface of the abdomen ; k,
posteriors ; l, umbilical cord ; m, umbilical vesicle.

296 Natural size of a human embryo 4 weeks old.

297 Magnified appearance of a human embryo
4 weeks old—a, quadrigemina vesicle ;
b, cerebellum ; c, hemispheres ; d, eyes ;
e, rudiments of the upper jaw ; f, rudi-

ments of the tongue; *g*, rudiments of the lower jaw; *h*, rudiments of the tongue bone; *i*, heart; *k*, oblong marrow, or medulla oblongata; *l*, surface of the abdomen; *m*, upper extremities beginning to appear; *n*, lower extremities; *o*, the posteriors; *p*, part of the umbilical cord; *q*, posterior view of the vertebral column.

298 Natural size of a human embryo, in the 5th week of pregnancy.

299 Magnified appearance of a human embryo 5 weeks old—*a*, corpora quadrigemina; *b*, cerebellum; *c*, eyes; *d*, hemispheres; *e*, rudiments of the upper jaw; *f*, rudiments of the tongue; *g*, rudiments of the lower jaw; *h*, rudiments of the tongue bone; *i*, heart; *l*, upper extremities; *m*, lower extremities; *n*, surface of the abdomen.

300 A human embryo in the 6th week of pregnancy—natural size.

301 Magnified appearance of a human embryo 6 weeks old—*a*, corpora quadrigemina; *b*, cerebellum; *c*, oblong marrow; *d*, eyes; *e*, hemispheres; *f*, rudiments of the upper jaw; *g*, rudiments of the tongue; *h*, rudiments of the lower jaw; *i*, rudiments of the tongue bone; *k*, heart; *l*, umbilical cord; *m*, upper extremities; *n*, posterior view of the vertebral column; *o*, rudiments of the legs; *p*, posteriors.

301*a* Human embryo in the 7th week of pregnancy—natural size.

301*b* Magnified appearance of a human embryo 7 weeks old—*a*, corpora quadrigemina ; *b*, hemispheres ; *c*, cerebellum ; *d*, place where the neck detaches itself from the head ; *e*, rudiments of the upper jaw; *f*, part of the nose; *g*, rudiments of the tongue, already attached to each other ; *h*, cavity of the mouth ; *i*, rudiments of the lower jaw ; *k*, rudiments of the tongue bone ; *l*, supposed rudiments of the clavicle ; *m* and *n*, the auricles ; *o* and *p*, the ventricles of the heart; *q*, upper extremities ; *r*, lower extremities ; *s*, vertebral column ; *t*, umbilical cord ; *u*, the posteriors.

302 A human embryo in the 8th week of pregnancy—natural size.

303 Magnified appearance of a human embryo 8 weeks old—*a*, hemispheres ; *b*, corpora quadrigemina; *c*, fontanel ; *d*, cerebellum *e*, medulla oblongata; *f*, *g*, nostrils; *h*, rudiments of the upper jaw ; *i*, bridge of the nose; *k*, rudiments of the lower jaw ; *l*, ears; *m*, heart; *n*, liver; *o*, intestines ; *q*, the upper extremities ; *r*, surface of the abdomen ; *s*, vertebral column ; *t*, lower extremities ; *u*, sexual organs.

304 Human embryo, in the 9th week of pregnancy—natural size.

305 Magnified appearance of a human embryo 9 weeks old—*a*, hemispheres ; *d*, corpora quadrigemina ; *c*, first appearance of the fontanel; *d*, cerebellum; *e*, oblong marrow;

f, nostrils; *g*, rudiments of the upper jaw; *h*, indication of the canal of separation; *i*, the part of the nose attached to the middle rudiments, thus forming the nostrils; *k*, under lip, formed by the lower jaw; *l*, auditory vesicle; *m*, heart; *n*, liver; *o*, œsophagus; *p*, upper extremities; *q*, lower extremities; *r*, fingers; *s*, articulations of the arm; *t*, toes; *v*, articulations of the knee; *w*, abdominal region; *x*, vertebral column.

306 A human embryo in the 10th week of pregnancy—natural size.

307 Magnified appearance of a human embryo 10 weeks old—*a*, hemispheres; *b*, corpora quadrigemina; *c*, cerebellum; *d*, ear; *e*, hand; *f*, ribs; *g*, position of the liver; *h*, umbilical cord; *i*, vertebral column; *k*, posteriors.

308 A human embryo in the 11th week of pregnancy—natural size.

309 Magnified appearance of a human embryo 11 weeks old—*a*, hemispheres; *b*, fontanel; *c*, frontal bone; *d*, position of the abdomen; *e*, umbilical cord; *f*, sexual parts; *g*, fold of the skin for the two lips of the pudendum, or for the testicles; *h*, anus.

310 A human embryo 3 months old—*a*, amnion; *b*, chorion; *c*, umbilical cord; *d*, villi.

311 An embryo 13 weeks old. The ovum is broken and the membrane thrown back.

312 Human embryo 3½ months old. The ovum is broken, but the amnion, in which the

embryo is contained, is still closed.

313 An open womb, containing an embryo 5 months old. A portion of the deciduary membrane is shown : the embryo is in the amnion, which is surrounded by the villi ; the colour of vagina is changed ; the sexual parts are laid open, and visible on both sides.

314 An embryo of 4 months old laid open, showing the thoracic and abdominal cavities.

315 Magnified hand of an embryo 10 weeks old.

316	do.	do.	11	do.
317	do.	do.	·12	do.
318	do.	foot of do. ·	12½	do.

319 Magnified head of an embryo 13 weeks old.

320	do.	do.	14	do.

321 Sexual parts of an embryo 10 weeks old.

322	do.	do.	9	do. ⎞
323	do.	do.	12	do. ⎬ magnified
324	do.	do.	14	do.
325	do.	do.	15 ·	do. ⎠

326 A fœtus 7 months old.

327   do. 8   do.

328   do. 9   do.

———

The Development of the Face.

329 Head of embryo at the beginning of the third week of pregnancy—a, the hemispheres ; b, cavity of the palate ; c, the two parts which form the upper jaw ; d, the two parts which form the tongue ; ε, the two parts which form the lower jaw ; f, the two parts which form the tongue bone ; g, the heart.

330 Head of an embryo at the end of the fourth week of pregnancy—*a*, hemispheres; *b*, the parts which form the upper jaw; *c*, the cavity of the palate; *d*, the two parts which form the tongue; *e*, the two parts which form the lower jaw; *f*, the parts which form the tongue bone, half closed.

331 Head of a fœtus 6 weeks old—*a*, the hemispheres; *b*, rudiments of the upper jaw; *c*, tongue; *d*, tongue bone; *e*, lower jaw.

332 Head of a fœtus 7 weeks old—*a*, the hemispheres; *c*, small protuberances at the place of the closing parts, forming the upper jaw, and which afterwards form the nose; *c*, palate; *d*, tongue; *e*, lower jaw; *f*, tongue bone; *g*, auditory canal.

333 Head of a fœtus in the beginning of the 8th week—*a*, hemispheres; *b*, bridge of the nose; *c*, the base of the coming nostrils; *d*, the tongue; *e*, lower jaw; *f*, auditory passage; *g*, the palate.

334 Head of a fœtus at the end of the 8th week—*a*, the nostrils; *b*, base of the nostrils; *c*, the wings of the nose; *d*, tongue; *e*, lower jaw.

335 Head of a fœtus at the beginning of the 9th week—*a*, hemispheres; *b*, wings of the nose; *c*, nostrils; *d*, upper lip; *e*, upper jaw; *f*, bridge of the nose.

336 Head of a fœtus 9 weeks old—*a*, arch for the eyebrows; *b*, groves of the nose formed by the closing of the upper lip; *c*, beginning of the under lip, produced by the closing of the lower jaw.

337 Head of a fœtus, ten weeks old—*a*, hemispheres; *b*, arch for the eyebrows; *c*, lachrymal canal; *d*, folds, which are probably the stratum of the muscles; *e*, the ear. The face is formed in three months for all the rudiments are then developed, and the outlines are distinct.

The Development of the Genital Parts.

338 Genital organs of a fœtus 3 weeks old When the muscles of the abdomen become closed, there remains still a small opening, through which the genital parts are developed—*a*, issue of the intestines; *b*, posteriors.

339 Genital organs of a fœtus 4 weeks old. At this opening a small protuberance presents itself which serves to form the clitoris— *a*, clitoris; *b*, pudendum; *c*, posteriors.

340 Genital organs of a fœtus, 5 weeks old. The clitoris is here more developed, and the major and minor lips or labia are shown —*a*, clitoris; *b*, pudenda; *c*, nymphœ; *d*, posteriors.

341 Genital organs of a fœtus, 6 weeks old— *a*, clitoris; *b*, minor lips; *c*, major lips; *d*, proturbations which form the anus; *e*, posteriors.

342 Genital organs of a fœtus, 7 weeks old—*a*, clitoris; *c*, major lips; *c*, the two sides of this opening, which begin to unite and form the perineum; *d*, the perineum; *e*, posteriors.

343 Genital organs of a fœtus, 8 weeks old. The two sides here are united, and the perineum is formed—*a*, clitoris; *b*, minor lips; *c*, the perineum; *d*, the anus; *e*, posteriors.

344 Genital organs of a fœtus, 9 weeks old—*a*, clitoris; *b*, minor lips; *c*, major lips; *d*, perineum; *e*, anus; *f*, coccyx hardly visible.

345 Genital organs of a fœtus, 10 weeks old—*a*, clitoris; *b*, propuce; *c*, minor lips; *d*, major lips; *e*, vulva; *f*, perineum; *g*, anus.

346 Genital organs of a fœtus, 11 weeks old. It is only in the third month that the sex can be distinguished—*a*, penis; *b*, orifice of the urethra; *c*, prepuce; *d*, minor lips *e*, major lips, forming the scrotum; *f*, perineum; *g*, anus.

347 Genital organs of a fœtus, 12 weeks old. The testicles are closed, the penis still opened for the urine—*a*, aperture; *b*, prepuce; *c*, parts forming the urinary canal; *d*, the suture; *e*, the testicles; *f*, anus.

348 Genital organs of a fœtus, 13 weeks old. At three months and a half, the penis is quite closed; the last closing is called the frœnum—*a*, aperture; *b*, prepuce; *c*, suture.

352 Twins in the uterus, showing the natural position, eight months old.

636*a* A child born in proper time, attached to the placenta by the umbilical cord.

637 A model of the Chinese hetrodelph, A Kin. This extraordinary being was born with

the body of a second infant projecting from his chest, the two being firmly united at the sternum. He lived to reach the adult state, and having been first seen by a captain in the East India Company's service, was afterwards exhibited in London. These cases are exceedingly rare.

639 The bust of a young woman, representing a corpse. The fat yellow part in front of the neck is—*a*, the thyroid body. The chest being open shows—*b*, the heart in its natural position ; *c*, the great veins and arteries : *d*, the ramifications of the bronchi ; and *e*, the diaphragm, which separates the thoracic from the abdominal cavity. The expression of this face merits especial attention.

640 A man named Monsieur Duval, who is still living in the hospital of Val-de-Grace, in Paris, with an excrescence called *goitre*, which entirely surrounds his neck, measuring 60 inches in circumference, and weighing 20 pounds.

641 Portrait of a Swiss woman, affected with goitre, or wen.

643 Hair lip. In this is seen the result of arrested developement.

645 Part of the leg of a pregnant woman, showing the enormous enlargement of the blood-vessels, known under the name of varicose veins.

658 The disease called hæmorrhoids, or piles.

661 Intestinal hernia, or rupture in the region

of the inguinal ligament in man, which
can be taken to pieces.

662 Double intestinal rupture, which can also
be taken to pieces.

663 Inguinal and scrotal hernia.

Eye Diseases.

664 Eversion of the inferior
eyelid.

665 Syphilitic eruption of
the superior and in-
ferior eyelids, with
gonorrhœal opthal-
min.

666 Syphilitic eruption of
the superior eyelid
and eversion of the
inferior.

667 Opacity of the cornea.

668 Beginning of the formation of an ulcer in
the cornea.

669 Abscess of the cornea.

670 Opacity of the crystalline lens.

671 Iris, irregular and entirely discoloured.

672 Grey capsular cataract

673 Ditto ditto.

674 Four humid warts on
the iris.

675 Three ditto, ditto.

676 Gonorrhœal opthal-
mia.

677 Violent inflammation
of the iris.

678 Ulceration of the eyelid

679 Eversion of the eyelid

680 Blister and malignant
pustule of the su-
perior eyelid.

681 Hordeolum or stye, on
the upper eyelid.

Diseases of the Heart.

683 A heart affected with Pericarditis. This
disease, which consists of an inflammation
of the pericardium or membrane investing
the heart, is of a very dangerous character.
The membrane becomes preternaturally
red, coagulable lymph adheres to its surface, and there is an effusion of fluid into
its cavity. The redness is here shown on
one side, and the lymph on the other.

684 Pericarditis in a more advanced stage. The lymph is here thrown out in such quantities as to cause adhesion between the heart and the pericardium.

685 A heart affected with what is termed endocarditis, *i.e.*, inflammation of the lining membrane of the heart. As this membrane is folded at the inlets and outlets of the heart, to form the valves when it is affected, it is generally at the points nearest the valves. In this case a deposit consisting of three groups, will be observed on the tricuspid valve, and a large quantity on the mitral valve. The carneo columæ are also affected.

686 A further advanced stage of endocarditis, in which ossification of the mitral valve has taken place, together with great thickening of the walls of the left ventricle. This last is a most common result.

687 A model of a heart affected with fatty degeneration. In this disease, the whole muscular substance of the heart becomes converted into fat, the consequence of which is that rupture generally ensues, and the blood escapes into the surrounding cavity, as has occurred in this case.

Diseases of the Lung.

688 Inflammation of the substance of the lung.

689 Tubercular deposit infiltrated into the lung, bronchial tubes, &c. A fresh crop of tubercles is seen making their appearance.

783 Madame DIMAXCHE. This woman, who
lived not far from Paris, in the village of
Bercy, had in her 24th year, exostoses
and excrescences on different parts of her
body, like those on the right check : the
excrescence, or horn, which she had in the
middle of her forehead attained a length of
10 inches towards her 80th year: she was
operated on at Paris, by Dr. Souberbielle,
and lived about seven years after the
operation, by which she was quite cured.
The horn itself is still preserved, and may
be seen in the Museum Dupuytren, Paris.
784 Foot of a Chinese woman.

Dreadful Effects of Tight Lacing.
785 A magnificent full-length figure in wax of a
young lady of Munich, 18 years of age,
who, having from her earliest childhood
accustomed herself to the pernicious habit
of tight lacing, suddenly dropped down
dead in the arms of her partner while
dancing at a ball in her native city.
Mothers, daughters, wives, fathers, and
husbands have an equal interest in the
contemplation of this figure, as it truly
represents the direful consequences of a
submission to the capricious dictates of
fashion, in defiance of the laws of nature.
786 Represents her child in wax, as it is now
preserved in Munich.
787 The deformed thoracic cavity of the above.

788 The chest of a well-formed young woman
who has never worn stays; intended to
illustrate, by comparison, the horrible
compression of the thorax in the preceding model.

Surgical Operations.

789 Operation for hair lip. This consists in
paring the edges of the fissure, bringing
them together, and confining them with
sutures and bandages.
790 Operation for cataract. This model is a
figure of Catherine Bindermann, 22 years
of age, upon whom the operation was
performed in 1848, on both eyes, with
perfect success; on the left in May, and
on the right in July.
791 Operation for strabismus or squint.
792 Operation for fistula lachrymalis: This
disease consists in a stoppage of the duct
by which the tears are conveyed into the
nose.
793 Portrait of a young Hungarian nobleman,
upon whom the operation of tithotrity
was performed in the year 1843. Here
is viewed a successful case of crushing or
breaking the stone in the bladder, and
consequently its removal, without the
pain and danger of cutting.

Circumcision, as performed among the Jews.

This highly interesting operation, commanded by Divine authority thousands of years ago, and still performed by the decendants of the peoplo amongst whom it was first employed, consists of two parts; the one, that of removing the skin of the prepuce; and the other, the turning back a small portion of the remaining inner skin. It is performed on the eighth day, and is of much more importance than is generally imagined. Does he who scoffs at this operation know that some of these diseases of these parts are by it entirely avoided?—for example, phymosis and paraphymosis, for which, see Nos. 962 and 963

794 A model, showing the operation of circumcision.

The Rhinoplastic Operation.

795 The Talacotian, or Italian mode of performing the Rhinoplastic operation.
796 The Indian mode. In this model the flap is seen cut and partly turned round, so as to bring it down to form the nose.
797 The same operation, with the nose formed
798 The Rhinoplastic operation, with the parts shown nearly healed.

798a This figure represents the features of a lady at Paris, who submitted to the Cæsarian operation, and who is still living. The reason for its performance was the presentation of two children joined together. The expression of anxiety and extreme pain is represented in the figure—chloroform being at that time unknown.

The Human Brain compared with those of different Animals.

799 A cod's brain.
800 The brain of a two months' old fœtus resembling the preceding.
801 The left hemisphere of a crocodile's brain.
802 The brain of a three months' old fœtus, resembling the preceding.
803 The left hemisphere of a falcon's brain.
804 The brain of a four months' old fœtus, resembling the preceding.
805 The left hemisphere of a house-dog's brain.
806 The right hemisphere of the brain of a five months' old fœtus, resembling the preceding.
807 The right hemisphere of the brain of a six months' old fœtus, magnified.
808 The left hemisphere of the brain of a seven months' fœtus, magnified.
809 The right hemisphere of a human brain cut horizontally, so as to show the external structure.
810 Base of the brain and the tissue of the nerves
811 The interior of the right hemisphere of the brain.
812 The exterior of the right hemisphere of the brain.

The Teeth of the Horse as an index to Age.

It is a very ancient opinion, that the age of a horse may bo determined by an examination of its teeth, and one which time has only served to confirm. No doubt, in the majority of cases, this can be done most accurately, but, at the same time, it must be borne in mind, that there are cases in which the best and most experienced judges may be mistaken. The following series or models will illustrate the principle points to be observed : —

834 Teeth of the horse at nino months old ; the corner milk teeth are up, but their edges do not meet. The gums are much protruded at this age.

835 Teeth of tho horse at two years old. A full mouth of milk incisors, all of which show considerable wear.　　　　　　　D

837 The horse's mouth at three years old,
showing one of the lateral milk teeth
shed, and the permanent tooth coming up.

838 Mouth of the horse when rising four years;
the lateral horse teeth are in the mouth,
but their edges do not fairly meet.

839 Mouth of the horse when four years old,
showing four pairs of horse teeth well up,
but the corner milk teeth retained. This
appearance cannot well be mistaken.

840 Mouth of the horse when rising five years.
All the horse teeth are in the mouth, but
the corner teeth have not yet met.

841 Mouth of the horse at five years old, showing a full mouth of horse incisors, all the
edges of which fairly meet.

843 Mouth of the horse when six years old. The
corner teeth look more firmly set, and
their edges begin to be uneven; they have
become more square in the figure of the
external surface, the edges of the teeth
fairly meet when the mouth is closed, and
the round appearance of the posterior
border is nearly lost.

844 Mouth of the horse when seven years old.
The corner teeth exhibit further evidence
of wear.

————

*Models showing the Development of the Fowl
from the Egg.*

850 Hen, which can be taken to pieces, exhibiting the ovaries and the successive pro-
gression of the egg until the moment of
its issue.

851 to 872 Show the development of the chicken
from the first day of its incubation until
the twenty-second, when fully developed.

_____

*Microscopic Models illustrating the Development
of the Frog.*

873 An ovum from the spawn of the frog. There
is a striking peculiarity in these eggs,
• which is, that they are light on one side
and dark on the other, presenting two distinct hemispheres of different shades.

874
875
876
877
878
879
880

These seven models illustrate the changes
the egg undergoes after impregnation has
taken place. A fissure is first observed,
dividing the ovum externally into two,
these subdivided into four, the four into
eight, the eight into sixteen, then thirty-
two, sixty-four, and so it continues, until
the subdivisions are so minute as to be
scarcely perceptible. These changes take
place in about two hours. ·

881 After the previous changes have taken place
others may now be observed. The subdivisions having become so minute as to be
scarcely perceptible—on the first day, a
fissure may be seen, called the primitive
stripe. This is the commencement of the
development of the embryo.

882	Ovum on the second day.	886	Ovum on the sixth day.
883	do. third do.	887	do. seventh do.
884	do. fourth do.	888	do. eighth do.
885	do. fifth do.	889	do. ninth do.

In this last model it will be seen the tail of the young animal (for such it has now become) is slightly curved on one side ; by this means it breaks the case which enveloped it, and makes its escape into the water. It nas now become what is usually denominated a tadpole.

890
891
892
893
894
895
896
897
898

These nine models illustrate the further changes undergone by the embryonic frog. The tadpole having emerged from the egg, escapes into the water, where it lives the life of a fish, breathing water through its gills, having at that time no lungs, and being, therefore, incapable of breathing air. Further changes take place : its form becomes more definite ; then the openings on each side of its head close, the water can no longer pass through its gills ; lungs make their appearance, and the young reptile(for such it has now become) elevates its nose above the water, and inhales the air. Then small rudimentary extremities may be seen first behind, and then in front; these become longer and more fully developed, the tail disappears by the body growing over it, and the condition of the perfect frog is arrived at. The whole of these changes take about two months to accomplish.

OBSTETRIC PREPARATIONS.
Miniature Models illustrating the various Positions of the Child in the Womb and during Birth, together with the different stages of Delivery.

899 The mode of introducing the finger, for the purpose of ascertaining what part of the child is presenting.

900 Measuring the diameter of the pelvis with the finger, to ascertain whether there is room for the child to pass.

901 The head descending into the pelvis with the face directed backwards, and to the right side.

902 The head descending with the face directed backwards, and to the left side.

903 The head descending with the face directed forwards, and to the right side.

904 The head descending with the face directed forwards, and to the left side.

905 Face presentation.

906 The method of introducing the finger, fo. the purpose of rupturing the membranes, and allowing the waters to escape.

907 This model shows the extraordinary elasticity of the perineum, and how it becomes expanded during the descent of the child.

908 One foot having presented, the leg has descended, leaving the other directed upwards, in contact with the body.

909 A transverse presentation, the left arm descending.

N.B.—In cases of this kind the operation of turning the child will have to be resorted to before the labour can be accomplished.

910 Delivery in the sitting posture: a mode adopted in some of the continental countries.

911 Delivery on the left side, with a pillow between the knees: the mode adopted in this country.

912 The abdomen presenting, with the descent of the umbilical cord, and the womb contracted upon the child.

913 The mode of arranging the fingers, when it may be necessary to introduce the whole hand.

914 Mode of bringing down the legs in a breech presentation.

915 The operation of turning, for the purpose of bringing down the head.

916 The operation of turning, for the purpose of bringing down the feet

917 Transverse presentation, the back of the child laying over the mouth of the womb. The hand of the accoucheur is introduced for the purpose of turning.

918 Turning by grasping the feet of the child and bringing them down.

919 Turning, for the purpose of converting a transverse presentation into a longitudinal one.

920 Attaching a loop of cord to the feet of the child, for the purpose of bringing them down.

921 The feet having been brought down are being drawn through the mouth of the womb.

922 Bringing the body of a child through the pelvis in a foot presentation.

923 Bringing down the shoulders in a foot presentation.

924 Extracting the head in a foot presentation.

925 Removing the head completely out of the pelvis.

926 Bringing away the placenta, the hand having hold of the umbilical cord.

927 Detaching the placenta where it may be adhering to the womb.

928 A peculiar contraction in the middle of the womb, called the "Hour-Glass Contraction."

929 The placenta presenting, or what is called placenta prœvia.

N.B.—These cases are very dangerous; the bleeding is generally excessive.

———

929*a* Foot presentation.—Here the child makes its exit from the womb by the feet, instead of the head; a running knot is attached to the left hand of the fœtus, for the purpose of assisting delivery.

929*b* A preparation representing the left hand introduced, in order to disengage the placenta.

929*c* Breech presentation.—In this abnormal accouchement the child comes out the breech first, the infant's legs are bent upon the chest. The delivery is obtained by means of a blunt hook; and the child is usually much injured by this kind of operation.

929*d* Forceps delivery.—In many accouchements the instrument called forceps is used to disengage the head of the child. This operation, however, is not so dangerous as would appear by this model.

929e Transverse position of the child.—In this case the child must be turned in the accouchement; for this purpose the accoucher's hand is introduced, to effect the turning by means of the feet.

929f Face presentation.—Here, instead of the face being turned to one side, it is presenting; and in order to prevent the rupture of the perineum, the hand is placed beneath for its support.

———

THE GENERATIVE ORGANS AND DISEASES CONSEQUENT UPON THE INFRINGMENTS OF CHASTITY.

Most of the specimens in this series are actually copied from morbid appearances, and are not in the slightest degree exaggerated. Dr. Kahn's wish in exhibiting them is not to gratify a prurient curiosity but to present the scientific observer with a general and correct view of the perfect and wonderful structure of the human frame, and to point out the direful consequences attending any departure from the unerring and beneficent laws ordained by the Creator for the government and propagation of the human race.

930 A back view of the male organs of generation—a, bladder; b, spermatic artery, vein and nerve; c, testicle; d, e, tubuli seminiferi; f, g, h. epididymis; i, vas deferens; j, vesiculæ seminals; k, prostate gland; l, urethra; m, Cowper's gland; n, bulb of the urethra; o, the erector muscles; p, q, veins and arteries of the penis, called dorsal; r, integument

underneath the penis; *s*, gland penis; *t*,
orifice; *u*, raphe, which joins the anus;
v, *w*, cremaster muscle; *y*, *z*, ureters.

932 Double penis, taken from a model in King's
College Hospital. The man is believed
to be still living in London.

933 The internal sexual parts in a state of
virginity—*a*, external labia; *b*, internal
labia; *c*, clitoris; *d*, entrance to the bladder; *e*, entrance to the vagina, which,
in virginity, is partially closed by a membrane called hymen, *f*, whose absence,
however, is not by any means a proof of
unchastity, as it is sometimes deficient
from infancy, and at other times so slight
as to be ruptured by ordinary exertion.

934 By this model is represented an elongated
clitoris, as seen in a girl still living in
Munich, and who, since the age of eight
years, had practised onanism, or self-
abuse, to such an extent, that the clitoris
had become enlarged.

935 Another case of elongation of the clitoris.

936 A Hottentot woman with an enormous clitoris. It is said that women of that race pur-
posely elongate the clitoris themselves and
mutually satisfy their sexual propensities.

939 Elephantiasis of the female sexual parts,
the result of onanism.—*See Appendix*.

940 Elongation and varicocele of the left testicle,
with diminution of the sexual organs, the
common result of self-abuse.—*See Appendix*.

941 Elongation and varicocele of both testicles the result of onanism.—*See Appendix.*

9:2 The same parts after treatment.

945 Testicle laid open, showing varicocele.

946 The external appearance of the above.

946a Another model showing varicocele.

947 Spinal cord diseased by the effects of onanism, taken from a boy 12 years of age, who died in the hospital at Vienna.

948 Sexual parts of an individual, who is still living in Paris: the scrotum is split, the penis like the clitoris of a woman, joined to the scrotum without being pierced: the evacuation of the urine is by an opening resembling a vagina, which is seen beneath the sexual parts.

949 Sexual parts of an individual named Gottlich, born near Dresden, in Saxony: his scrotum consists of two equal parts: instead of the penis there is a species of clitoris, beneath which is found an opening two inches deep, by which the urine is evacuated.

950 Sexual parts of an individual named Sandl, who is still living in Brunswick: his penis is very short and not pierced: the urine is evacuated by an opening in the scrotum, which is split.

9:1 Prolapsus Uteri.—This malady occurs to women who have had many children and those of a weak constitution who are obliged to stand long in an upright position.

Venereal Disease.

The question will naturally arise, on viewing a collection of this description, as to what its effect may be upon the minds of the rising generation. The mode hitherto adopted in the education of youth has been to keep them in perfect ignorance of the perils which await them during the critical passage from adolescence to manhood. The evil results of this system have been shown by the destruction of many a promising young man, who, had he the least idea of the probable consequences of an illicit indulgence of his passions might have brought reason to his aid, and resisted those temptations to which he, unfortunately, became a prey. "Forewarned, forearmed," is a good motto; and Dr. Kahn trusts that the horrible results of vicious indulgence, as shown in the following collection, will contribute as much to the promotion of morality and chastity, if not more, than the most earnest parental admonition.

or even the solemn warnings from the pulpit. The gradations of these diseases are here faithfully delineated, and it is necessary to add that they are all models of real cases, and are not in the slightest degree exaggerated.

957 Chordee, the result of gonorrhœa; also showing the perulent discharge.

958 Section of the penis showing the manner in which gonorrhœa affects the urethra.

959 Section of the penis, showing stricture of the urethra, the result of the indiscriminate use of injections.

959a Commencement of a stricture in the urethra.

959b A small stricture, caused by an injection of nitrate of silver.

959c Progress of a stricture.

959d Further progress of a stricture.

959e Mode of introducing a bougie in stricture of the urethra.

960 Venereal ulcer at the commencement of the urethra.

961 Malignant gonorrhœa, with the foreskin contracted behind the gland: this is called paraphymosis.

962 Operation for phymosis. This disease is caused by a chancre behind the corona glandis. The operator endeavours to force the foreskin over the gland.

963 Operation for paraphymosis. This is caused by a stricture of the foreskin. There the operator has recourse to the lancet, and makes an incision in the foreskin.

964 Ten syphilitic ulcers or cancers on the prepuce and glands.

965 Destruction of the foreskin, exposing the gland, the result of neglecting phymosis.

966 Cancer of the penis. In this case the amputation of the entire penis was necessary.

967 Inflammation of the scrotum, frequently the result of gonorrhœa when too quickly stopped by maltreatment. Several abscesses are formed in the scrotum.

968 Gangrene and mortification of the scrotum, with partial destruction of the skin of the penis, which occurred during a course of mercury, administered to cure an inguinal bubo on the right side.

970 Hydrocele, or water in the testicle, with application of the trochar.

971 Amputation of the penis, caused by gangrene and mortification.

972 Abscess of the outer lip on the left of the pudendum, as well as many chancres at the two exterior lips.

973 Two tumours in the inguinal region, of the size of an egg, called buboes.

974 Pointed warts on the great lips.

975 Vulva almost entirely destroyed by chancres.

976 Venereal disease in the parts of an individual who lived near Munich, and who was regarded as a woman until he attained his 20th year. For two years he had cohabited as a female; but having caught the venereal disease in the month of January, 1850, he was brought to Munich, and at the hospital of that town was declared to be of the masculine gender.

B 3

977 By the application of the speculum to this
figure, many chancres are seen in the
vagina, and at the mouth of the womb.
978 Syphilitic eruptions on the palm of the
hand, taken from the work of M. Ricord,
plate xxvi., pub. 1840.
979 Pemphigus syphiliticus on the sole of the
foot, from M. Ricord's plate xxv. Communicated by Dr. Cuillier, June, 1844.
979a Two buboes, one broken, the other not,
but much inflamed.
979c Schirrhous enlargement of the testicle.
979d Vegetations on and round the glans penis.
979e Schirrhous disease seen after an incision
made in the prepuce, showing ulceration
of the glans.
979f Gonorrhœa in the female.
979g Humid warts on the perineum.
979h A number of humid warts, covering all
the exterior part of the pudendum.
979i Lenticular ulcers, with humid warts of the
anus and its environs.
979j Aggravated syphilitic ulcerations and commencement of mortification.

Syphilis in the Face.

980 Venereal ulcers on the tongue and underlip
in a young woman at Manchester, arising
from the shuttle, employed in weaving,
accidentally striking her in the mouth,
the shuttle having been previously used
by a person suffering from syphilis.

981 Venereal ulcers on the underjaw and lip, arising from smoking a pipe which had previously been used by a person affected with syphilis.

982 Chancre in the superior lip, as well as the inferior, with loss of incisor teeth : result of caries of the upper jaw.

983 A negro with caries of the frontal bone, and an exostosis on the right side of the superior jaw.

984 Syphilitic eruption of the skin, extending all over the body.

985 The soft and hard parts of the nose destroyed and the left eye attacked, the result of the indiscriminate use of mercury.

985a Scabbypustules and corny ulcers, with concrete secretions over the body.

986 The roof of the palate destroyed and ulceration of the inner canthus of the eye, in a young woman 23 years old.

987 A young girl aged 18 years with syphilitic eruptions all over the body.

988 Woman 24 years old, having the frontal bone attacked with caries, the result of improper use of mercury.

989 Total loss of the nose and its environs, which occurred to a girl aged 19.

990 Woman 25 years old, who persisted in concealing a syphilitic complaint, so that ultimately she entirely lost her nose and half of the superior jaw.

992 Salivation, the terrible result of the injudicioususeof mercuryintreatmentofdisease.

993 Head of a child born of syphilitic parents, with congenital chancres on the lips.

994 Breast of a woman who became affected with secondary symptoms, by suckling the preceding case.

995 An extraordinary model, showing the whole of the contents of the abdominal and thoracic cavities, the walls being removed, the viscera are exposed on all sides—1, the tongue; 2, larynx; 3, trachea; 4, thyroid gland; 5, vena cava superior; 6, aorta; 7, heart; 8, 8, lungs; 9, diaphragm; 10, liver; 11, gall-bladder; 12, stomach; 13, spleen; 14, small intestines; 15, transverse colon; 16, bladder; 17, penis; 18, testes; 19, vasa deferentia; 20, prostate gland; 21, seminal vesicles; 22, rectum; 23, pharynx; 24, œsophagus; 25, descending aorta; 26, inferior vena cava; 27, kidneys; 28, supra venal capsules.

996 A model showing the disease termed Keloide affecting the left breast of a young female, a native of Vienna. This disease is of rare occurrence—was first described by Albert under the name of Cancroide—and is termed by the French ' Dartre de graisse.' It commenced in this case with a pain in the breast, then a small spot appeared the size of a fourpenny piece; this gradually became larger, and ultimately a long band of tissue became affected, presenting the appearance of a burn; the pain became

sharp, and occurred at regular intervals of
15 days. The case was cured in a month.

997 The fingers affected with what is termed
Onychia, a disease consisting of ulceration at the root of the nail, either of the
fingers or toes. It commences with a
swelling, of a deep red colour, and the
oozing of a thin ichor from under the
fold of skin at the root of the nail; and
ultimately an ulcer is formed from which
issues a fœtid sanious discharge. The
disease is extremely painful, more particularly during the night. In this case it
arose, as it sometimes does, from syphilis.

998 The sexual organs of a Hottentot female,
showing what is termed the natural apron.

999 The brain, with the spinal cord, showing
the origin of the various cerebral and
spinal nerves.

1000 Model of a child affected with syphiltic
pemphigus. This case, notwithstanding
the general medical opinion that the
disease when it occurs in this form is incurable, is of a most interesting character.
The father had suffered much from the
venereal disease before marriage, and
had probably primary symptoms upon
him at the time this event took place. In
consequence of this the mother also became tainted. About a year after marriage
the child was born, and the face, hands and
feet were found covered with large blebs,
about the size of a walnut. For the first

year all sorts of remedies were tried, but
without effect. The general health of the
child then began to be effected, and the
febrile symptoms became dangerous. At
this time Dr. Kahn first saw the case, and
by a regular course of internal remedies,
and medicinal baths externally, a cure
was completed in a few weeks. The child
is now seven years of age, and has had no
recurrence of the symptoms.

1001 The Acarus Scabei, male and female.
One of the most important discoveries in
medical science that has recently been
made, is that the terrible and disgusting
disease called, in vulgar parlance, the
Itch, owes its existence to the work of a
small insect, which burrows under the
skin, and produces the discoloration and
irritation so tormenting to the patient.
The acarus has eight legs on the abdomen, covered with hair, four in front and
four behind, the former being furnished
with suckers. The back is armed with
short spears. It is exceedingly agile, runs
very fast, but does not jump, as was at
one time supposed. The front legs are
united by a web similar to that on the
duck's feet. The head is nodulated. The
male is but half the size of the female, and
is by many supposed to be alone capable
of burrowing into the skin. This animal
makes a small hole in the skin, and disappears, then burrows along a considerable

distance, the course it has taken being indicated by the change of colour on the out-
side (*A* represents the male, *B* the female)

1002 Model of an infant's arm, showing the
three punctures, as usually made in the
operation of vaccination.

1003 } Two similar models, showing different
1004 } stages of the action of the vaccine matter.

1005 Model of a child whose left arm shows cul-
mination of the effect of the vaccine matter, and the right arm the gradual drying
up of the pustules.

1006 Model of a head, showing the direful
ravages of the small-pox when the vaccine operation has not been performed.

1019 The larynx, with the windpipe; the bronchi
and the bronchial tubes. It opens, to
show the vocal chords.

1020 Illustration of the character of the remarkable and fatal disease Diphtheria.
This disease originates in a peculiar acute
inflammation of the mucous membrane
of the throat, producing a pseudo membrane, which rapidly enlarges, and results
in gangrene and suffocation.

1021 Ulcerations and vegetations of the pharynx
with hypertrophy of the mucous glands
and papillæ, resulting from syphilis
treated with excess of mercury.

1022 An arm bone, showing the fearful results
of mercurial treatment, the bone gradually
becoming spongiform and rotten.

———

1023 Stricture of the œsophagus from simple
inflammation, just below the bulb of the
larynx—*a*, the tongue; *b*, epiglottis; *c c*,
part of tharynx; *d*, larynx; *e*, the stricture; *g g*, thyroid gland; *h*, portion of
œsophagus below stricture; *i*, the trachea.

1024 An extensive contraction of the calibre of
the œsophagus, throughout nearly the
whole course of the tube—*a*, uvula; *b*,
tongue; *c*, epiglottis; *d*, thyroid gland;
e e e e, the thickened walls of the œsophagus, giving rise to the contraction.

1025 This figure represents a pouch which had
been formed in the lower end of the
pharynx by a cherry stone having rested
there, for three days, and formed a little
recess for itself. This recess was gradually
enlarged during the course of five years
by a part of the food constantly passing
into it, and for some time remaining in
it, till it arrived at the size represented.
The food at last was all detained in the
pouch or bag, and none of it passed into
the œsophagus—*a*, epiglottis; *b*, passage
to the trachea; *c*, that part of the pharynx
lying next to the larynx; *d*, the lower end
of the pouch; *e*, part of the œsophagus.

1026 The thyroid gland, much enlarged.

1027 In this figure will be seen a half-crown
piece which lodged in the œsophagus or
food pipe, causing death to the patient
within a few days. The surface of the
coin was found to be blackened by the
juices secreted in the mouth and œsophagus. The œsophagus is sometimes so large
in the adult as to allow a half-crown to
pass through it without injury, and afterwards escape by the rectum. A half-
crown which had made this journey was
preserved in Dr. Hunter's Museum.

1028 A portion of a tubular polypus, which had
been coughed up from the trachea.

1029 Outward appearance of an aneurism of the
arch of the aorta—b, the aorta ; c, the
aneurismal bag, arising from the arch.

1032 Preparation showing the right and left
lung ; on one side are shown the ramifications of the bronchial tubes, on the other
the distribution of arteries and veins.

1033 Inflammation of the substance of the lung
(pneumonia)withenlargementoftheorgan

1034 A section of the anterior part of right lung,
displaying the three degrees of peripneu-
mony, and uncircumscribed gangrene—
a b, the first degree (engorgement) ; b c,
the second degree (hepatization) ; c d, & e
f, the third degree (purulent infiltration) ; d e, gangrene.

1035 Tubercular cavern, half divided and

thrown open. Its walls exhibit external and internal thickening of the pleura, chronic grey induration and tubercles.

1036 Section of a lung, showing pulmonary apoplexy, the result of alcoholic excess.

1037 Portion of the lung of a person affected by asthma.

1038 Disease of the lungs, produced by inhalation of coal-dust (*colliers' phthysis*).

1039 Portion of a lung, showing dilitation of the bronchial tubes. A pin is passed through three which communicate. From ten years of asthma.

1040 Lungs and heart of a victim of pulmonary consumption. Tubercular deposits are seen upon the surface of the lungs, and even upon the heart.

1041 Lungs which have become ossified. A very rare diseased appearance—a, the trachea; b b, the two bronchi; c c c c c, the ossified portions of the lungs.

1045 Digestive apparatus, showing the whole course of the alimentary canal—a, the tongue; b, uvula; c, pharynx; d, trachea; e, œsophagus; f, thyroid gland; g, stomach; h, liver; i, gall-bladder; k, spleen; l, pancras; m, duodenum; n, small intestines; o, mesentery; p, cœcum; q, appendix vermiformis; r, ascending colon; s, transverse colon; t, descending colon; u, rectum; v, anus.

1046 Stomach, the front wall of which is removed,

showing its internal surface, &c.—*a*, termination of the food pipe into the stomach; *b*, passage from the stomach to the first portion of the small intestines; *c*, internal surface of the duodenum; *d*, small opening through which the gall and the pancreatic juice enters the duodenum; *e*, the pancreatic gland; *f*, the spleen.

1047 Model of the human stomach, showing the red suffusion and arborescent injection of acute inflammation of the serous membrane, and also a deposition of fibrine on the surface of the stomach, caused by excessive indulgence in alcoholic drinks—*a*, thoracic portion of œsophagus; *b b b*, portions of the fibrine; *c*, engorged state of veins of stomach; *d*, pyloric extremity of stomach, entering into *e*, the duodenum.

1048 Diffuse redness of the fundus of the stomach, excited by arsenic.

1049 The stomach of a musician; it was so diseased by intemperance, that it could scarcely retain two tablespoonfuls of soup.

1049*a* Appearance presented by the interior of the same stomach.

1050 Stomach of a shoemaker in Munich, who suffered from pains in the abdomen for many years, found after death to arise from a cancerous tumour in the stomach.

1051 Stomach of a boy 13 years of age, named Bissieux, who died at Rouen in France, and in which on *post mortem* examination being made by Dr. Blanche, a monstrosity resembling a fœtus was found adhering to its sides. The original preparation is still preserved in the Musèe Dupuytren, Paris.

1052 Preparation showing the under surface of the liver, gall-bladder, &c.

1053 Portion of the liver, showing hypertrophy of the white substance (called nutmeg liver), from an individual addicted to excessive drinking.

1054 Hard tubera on the surface of the liver, also from an individual addicted to excessive alcoholic drinking.

1055 A portion of the liver studded with tubercles.

1056 A part of the intestines, studded on the internal surface with tubercular deposits.

1057 Another part of the same, where the external surface is covered with tubercles.

1058 A gall-bladder, completely filled with gall-stones.

1059 The biliary ducts of the gall-bladder much enlarged, and a gall-stone ready to drop into the cavity of the duodenum—a, ductus hepaticus enlarged; b, the gall-stone ready to be discharged into c, the duodenum.

1060 External view of the anus, with three considerable tumours which are piles.

1061 The inner membrane of the anus dissected, bringing into view some varicose veins of a considerable size, demonstrating the true nature of piles.

1062 Stricture in the rectum about two inches

above the anus, occasioned by a schirrhous thickening of its coats—a, rectum, above the stricture, in a sound condition, but enlarged on account of the accumulation of the fœces above the stricture; b, the part where the stricture is; c, part of rectum under stricture; d, the anus.

1063 Fistula in ano—a, external opening of a fistula, through which a probe has been passed; b, the fistula, which is about two inches in length; a very small canal communicates with it, in which a bristle has been put, and very near its internal extremity there is an opening marked c, by which it communicates with the cavity of the rectum.

1070 Section of the human kidney, with a portion of ureter in a healthy condition.
1071 Kidney, with the arteries and veins injected.
1072 Bladder, prostate gland and vasa deferentia —a, bladder; b, prostate gland; c, seminal vesicle.
1073 Section of a kidney, where a calculus of a considerable size had grown in the pelvis of its ureter—a, the body of the stone brought into view by a portion of the pelvis of the ureter being removed.
1073a This model represents some further changes in the kidney and the pelvis of the ureter, from a stone having been long resident in the pelvis—a, the stone.
1074 A kidney much enlarged, and converted

into a number of cells. In consequence of the urine being accumulated above, a large stone lodged in its pelvis. A number of openings are made, in order to show the cells and the thinness of the substance—*a*, the stone.

1075 Section of the urinary bladder of an adult, showing a number of small calculi lodged in pouches within the bladder—*a a*, the calculi; *b*, considerable projection of an enlarged prostrate gland into the cavity of the bladder.

1076 Outer surface of the most common calculus.

1077 Section of the above.

————

1081 Female breast, or mammary gland, laid open so as to show its structure. The red vessels are the arteries, the blue ones the veins, and the white ones the lactiferous vessels, carrying the milk from all parts of the breast to the nipple.

1082 Breast with extra nipples. This occasionally happens; and considerable difficulty is sometimes experienced in detecting the true from the false nipples. After confinement, however, the flow of milk to the true nipple almost invariably indicates its position, and the extraneous ones may then be removed.

1083 Cancer of the breast.

1084 Section of the womb, exhibiting the enlarged state of the uterine vessels during menstruation

1085 Cancer of the womb.

1086 Ovarian conception.—A woman, 29 years of age died in Munich, in 1849, from the consequence of this abnormal conception; which is happily of very rare occurrence. On dissection of the body, a fœtus of four months old was found in the left ovary.

1087 Sexual parts of a woman, in whom, after death, it was found that a separation existed in the vagina, dividing it longitudinally into two parts.

1088 The uterus of a woman who had two children, with a difference of four weeks between the birth of each. On dissection, a septum was found to exist in the vagina; and there were two distinct wombs, thus accounting for this extraordinary phenomenon.

1089 Natural pelvis of the female, to which are attached the external and internal organs of generation, the fore-finger of the accoucheur being introduced for examination of the mouth of the womb. The uterus being laid open, shows a fœtus of three months old within it.

Series of models showing mechanical obstacles which sometimes impede or prevent impregnation in the female:

1090 An unusual stricture in the vagina—*a*, uterus; *b*, the stricture; *c*, part of the vagina above the stricture; *d*, part of the vagina below the stricture.

1091 Pedunculated tumour of the uterus, filling up the orifice of the womb. The largest known, as recorded by Dr. J. W. Francis, weighed 101 lbs.—*a*, uterus; *b*, the tumour.

1092 Model of the uterus in its normal condition, slightly magnified, divided longitudinally to show its interior cavity—*a*, part of the vagina; *b*, mouth of the womb; *c c c*, the walls of the womb; *d*, triangular cavity of the womb; the fissure from *b* to *d* indicates the canal of the cervix.

1093 Longitudinal division of the uterus, showing the canal of the cervix nearly obliterated, in which case, semen being prevented from entering the cavity of the womb, impregnation would be impossible.

1094 Longitudinal division of the uterus, showing the canal of the cervix much enlarged. Here the result would be, not only that the semen would not be retained in the womb, so as to fertilise the ovum, but the ovum itself would be soon carried away by the mucous secretions.

1095 Female pelvis, showing an abnormal obliquity of the uterus, of which there are endless varieties. These obliquities not only affect the functions of the uterus, but also seriously militate with the healthy action of the rectum and bladder, as it presses upon the one or the other —*a*, the reversed uterus, pressing against *b*, the rectum; *c*, the vagina; *d*, the bladder.

1095a Another model, illustrative of the obliquity of the uterus, described in the foregoing.

1096 Female pelvis, showing that displacement or falling of the womb, called prolapsus uteri.

1197 Represents a complete prolapsus of the uterus, with vagina inverted.

———— •

Five miniature models of the female figures, showing the alterations produced in all the external parts of the body by impregnation.

1098 Appearance at the end of the second month.
1099 Appearance at the end of the fourth month.
1100 Appearance at the end of the fifth month.
1101 Appearance at the end of the eighth month.
1102 Appearance at the end of the ninth month.

————

Series of models showing the gradual alterations which the mouth of the womb undergoes during gestation—in impregnation for the first time.

1103 The mouth of the womb previous to impregnation.
1104 A section of the preceding.
1105 Mouth of the womb in the third month.
1106 Mouth of the womb in the fifth month.
1107 Section of the preceding.
1108 Mouth of the womb in the sixth month.
1109 Section of the preceding.
1110 Mouth of the womb in the eighth month.
1111 Section of the preceding.

1112 Mouth of the womb during the first period
of labour, the opening being considerably
enlarged, showing part of the "amnion,"
in which the child is enveloped.

1113 Section of the preceding.

1114 Mouth of the womb in the second period
of labour, still further enlarged.

*Series of models showing the gradual alterations
which the mouth of the womb undergoes during
gestation—when the person has previously given
birth to a child.*

1115 Mouth of the womb before impregnation.

1116 Mouth of the womb in the third month.

1117 Mouth of the womb in the fifth month.

1118 Mouth of the womb in the sixth month;
the finger of the accoucheur introduced.

1119 Mouth of the womb in the seventh month,
partly in section ; the finger of the accoucheur introduced.

1120 Mouth of the womb in the eighth month,
partly in section; the finger of the accoucheur introduced.

1121 Section of the mouth of the womb in the
ninth month.

1122 Section of the mouth of the womb during
the second period of labour.

1123 Mouth of the womb three days after the
delivery of a child.

1130 to 1134 Five preparations showing the
early stages of incubation in the hen's egg.

Models of the male organs of generation, in health and in disease.

1140 Natural preparation of the penis, bladder, and seminal vessels, dried and injected—*a*, glans penis; *b b*, cavernous bodies, which are of a spongy structure. When the cells are filled with blood, the penis is in an erected state; *c*, the urethra surrounded by the corpus spongiosum; *d*, bulbous part of the urethra; *e*, bladder, extended; *f f*, seminal vessels; *g*, prostate gland.

1141 Penis laid open, showing strictures in the urethra—*a*, small portion of the bladder; *b b*, section of the prostate gland; *c c*, the corpora cavernosa; *d d*, the glans penis; *e e*, stricture near the orifice; *f f*, stricture near the bulb, nearly an inch in length.

1142 Miniature model, showing a perpendicular section of the male pelvis—*a*, section of the kidney; *b*, ureter leading into *c*, the bladder; *d*, the urethra; *e*, cavernous portion of the penis in an erected state; *f*, glans penis; *g*, section of testicle; *h*, the vessel that conducts the semen from the testicle into *i*, the seminal vessels; *j j*, prostate gland; *k k*, the rectum; *l l*, the spinal marrow.

1143 A very uncommon lusus naturæ in the vesiculæ seminales. The two are joined together, forming an irregular mass, and want entirely the excretory ducts—*a*, posterior surface of the bladder; *b b*, the two ureters; *c*, vesiculæ seminales united in one.

1144 The left seminal vesicle afflicted with scrofula—*a*, external surface of the bladder; *b b*, the two ureters; *c c*, the vesiculæ seminales, the left containing scrofulous pus.

1145 Enlarged prostate gland, in which a bougie had been passed through a part of its substance, in an attempt to draw off the urine—*a*, portion of the penis with the urethra; *b b*, the two sides of the prostate gland much enlarged in size; *c*, urinal bladder; *d*, a quill inserted in the portion of the gland through which the the bougie had been forced.

1146 Model showing enlargement of the prostate gland—*a*, the scrotum and the testes drawn upwards, in order to show *b*, the enlarged prostate gland; *c*, the bulbous portion of the urethra.

1147 Ulcer in the prostate gland—*a*, urinal bladder; *b b*, seminal vesicles; *c*, the ulcer in the gland, which is much enlarged.

Models illustrative of Gout.

1161 Ear, showing small nodule of urate of soda on the edge of the helix; the only external evidence of chalk-stones visible throughout the body.

1162 Great toe, showing deposits of urate of soda on its surface, the neighbouring veins enlarged, and the whole toe inflamed.

1163 Miniature model of the arm of a gouty
man, in which chalk-stones had become
developed to an extreme degree.

1164 Section of a finger, showing the thin layer
of deposit on the articular cartilages, also
on the ligaments, causing anchylosis, and
extending towards the surface.

1165 Thin horizontal section of cartilage, from
a limb amputated in 1847, exhibiting the
crystaline character of urate of soda.

1166 Crystals of urate of soda, obtained by
evaporating watery solution of blood.

1167 Uric acid from the blood, crystalised on
fibres by the uric acid thread experiment.

1168 Oxalate of lime, crystallized on a fibre,
obtained from perspiration.

1169 Model of a boy six years of age. The abdomen is laid open, showing groups of
worms in the intestines, and also a scrofulous enlargement of the mesenteric glands.

₊ Many of the greatest medical authorities are of
opinion that the children of parents who have suffered
from syphilis will be most likely to be affected with
scrofula.

1170 Sectional life-size model of a female figure,
showing the whole of the internal viscera,
from the brain down to the digestive and
generative organism—a, that part of the
brain called the cerebrum ; b, ditto ditto,
called the cerebellum; c, the medulla
oblongata; d, spinal marrow ; e, pitituary
membrane (organ of smell) ; f, entrance
to the eustachian tube (leading from the

throat to the ear); *g*, tongue; *h*, uvula; *i*, trachea, or windpipe; *j*, thyroid gland; *k*, œsophagus, or food pipe; *l*, right lung; *m*, heart; *n*, aorta, or great artery; *o*, diaphragm (muscle separating the abdominal and thoracic cavities); *p*, liver; *q*, stomach; *r*, spleen; *s*, small intestines; *t*, large intestines; *u*, rectum; *v*, bladder; *w*, uterus, or womb, laid open, and containing an embryo of about ten weeks; *x*, vagina; *y*, os·pubis.

1171 Section of the male organs of generation in a healthy condition—*a a a*, the cavernous portion of the penis; *b b b*, the spongy portion of the penis, surrounding *c*, the urethra; *e*, the bladder; *ff*, prostate gland; *g*, seminal vessels; *h*, the common ejaculatory duct, a very minute passage, which serves to convey the seminal fluid from the seminal vessels through the prostate gland ·into the urethra; *i*, section of the rectum; *j*, anus.

172 Corresponding section of the male organs of generation in a disordered state, illustrating the principal cause of involuntary discharges of seminal fluid. The references are the same as in the last model. It will be seen, on reference to *h*, the ejaculatory duct, that it is in a dilated condition, and that consequently when the seminal vessels are acted on by pressure, either

from the bladder or the rectum, the seminal fluid would meet with no resistance in its passage through the duct, but at once readily escape into the urethra, and so out of the system. Such dilitations as that shown it this model are generally the result of certain abuses of the generative organs, particularly when practised in early youth, before the parts have been perfectly developed. The result of such an abnormal state of the organs would be a premature discharge of seminal fluid during intercourse, involuntary emissions during sleep, or when at stool or voiding urine; such losses as a matter of course ultimately proving highly detrimental to the system, both physically and mentally.

1173 Section of a female pelvis (*real*) showing the vagina, uterus and rectum, with the mode of introducing the finger of the accoucher for examination of the os uteri.

1174 This model shows a section of the brain, with congestion of the blood vessels, caused by repeated shocks to the nervous system in consequence of masturbation, and resulting in apoplexy and death.

1175 Atrophy, or diminution of the prostate and penis, caused by indulgence in the odious vice of Onanism.

1176 Ulceration of seminal vesicles and ejaculatory ducts, the effect of improper treatment with mercury.

1177 Inflammation of the bladder and enlargement of the prostate by improper treatment, causing spermatorrhœa.

1178 Spermatorrhœa caused by the irritation produced by ascarides (worms) in the anus.—Removed by the destruction of the ascarides.

1179 Spermatorrhœa produced by a mechanical obstacle to defecation.—*i.e.*, stricture of the anus.—As soon as the obstacle was removed the spermatorrhœa ceased, and all the symptoms arising from it disappeared.

1180 Spermatorrhœa—a few drops of seminal fluid passing from the urethra after the expulsion of the urine.

1181 Spermatorrhœa—the seminal fluid pressed involuntarily from the vesiculœ seminales by the pressure of the fœces.

1182 Spermatorrhœa caused by an inflammation of the rectum.—Removed by curing the inflammatory condition.

1183 Spermatorrhœa—efflux of blood following expulsion of urine in a case where Onanism had been practised to a very great extent.

N.B.—The nine preceding models are from cases which have recently occurred in Dr. Kahn's own practice, and which he was able to treat successfully.

EXTRACTS

FROM THE FORTY-SEVENTH EDITION OF

D R. K A H N'S

TREATISE

ON THE

PHILOSOPHY OF MARRIAGE.

☞ The Fiftieth Edition of the above-mentioned
work has been just published by J. ALLEN, Warwick
Lane, Paternoster Row, price One Shilling.—It may
be obtained of the Money Taker or Attendants, at
the Museum, price One Shilling ; or, can be forwarded,
post free, for 13 Stamps, or in enclosed envelope for
18 Stamps, direct from the Author, 3, Tichborne
Street, Haymarket, London,—W.

It has been sugested by many friends of Dr. KAHN, and many visitors to his Museum, that as the object of that Museum is to enable every one to become acquainted with the Laws of Health and the detrimental effects of neglecting them, the catalogue of its contents would bo greatly enhanced in value by the addition of a few extracts from his other publications. Acting on this suggestion, Dr. KAHN now appends a few portions from some of the chapters in his work on the Philosophy of Marriage, which tend to illustrate one of the most prolific causes which produce that multitude of wan countenances and feeble forms which we meet at every turn.

In the model No. 1172, as compared with the one preceding, is seen an abnormal condition of the generative organism, which is induced by the frightful and odious vice of self-pollution.

The following extract from Chapter V. of the Philosophy of Marriage will illustrate some of the sequæla of that horrible practice.

EXTRACTS FROM CHAPTER V.,

ON THE

"ABNORMAL CONDITIONS OF THE GENERATIVE ORGANS."

The consequences of the habit of self-abuse are far too numerous to be referred to in the limited space at my disposal, or to be discussed in the minute manner in which they are treated in my works written only for the Medical Profession; but as the most common one, and that from which several others frequently arise, viz., spermatorrhœa, will have a chapter devoted exclusively to it, all that I shall do in this chapter will be to notice very briefly the usual effects which ensue, more especially that called varicocele, or varicose veins in the testicle. Frequent and undue actions of an organ, no matter in what part of the body situated, will cause a greater flow of blood to that organ, and a change is consequently very likely to take place in the number and condition of the blood-vessels; this is what occurs in the testes of varicocele. From the continual excitement and constant action of the parts in the formation and emission of large quantities of seminal fluid, the veins become enormously distended, and apparently more numerous, and their coats thickened; the scrotum generally becomes elongated on the affected side, more frequently the left, but sometimes both; the folds disappear, and the whole organ hangs down in a pendulous state; sometimes the testicle wastes entirely away, and, as a matter of course, impotence, in many cases, incurable, is the result. Varicocele, I have found, in 99 cases out of 100, is an accompanying symptom of spermatorrhœa.

In case 997*, for example, the patient told me, in various letters describing his condition, that he had practised the habit of masturbation from the age of ten, as near as he could recollect, but thought it might probably have been earlier. It was first commenced by mere accident: Climbing a tree in his father's garden to obtain some fruit, the friction upon the genital organs produced so agreeable a sensation, that he repeated the act again and again; this led him to attempt to produce the same pleasurable feelings by other means. Having continued this practice for two or three years, and emissions occurring, he began to have inclinations for intercourse with the opposite sex, which this vicious practice was found the means of gratifying. At last, when about sixteen, he determined to discontinue the baneful practice, not because he saw any evil in it, but because he looked upon it as a boyish habit; and as he was now arriving, as

*It is requisite that I should say here, with regard to the introduction of illustrative cases, that in no instance whatever is any particular introduced, which can possibly lead to identification, and further that my case book is so full of such illustrative cases, treated long since, and wherein the parties have been fully restored, and are now beyond even suspicion of former evil of any kind, that there exists no necessity for making use of more recent instances.

he thought, at manhood, he concluded that the practices of children, this amongst the number, should be thrown aside; but before he had adhered to his resolution for a week, he was seized with an excessive desire for sexual intercourse; this, he said, he dared not indulge in for fear of violating those precepts of Christianity which his father had instilled into his mind. Fornication he looked upon as a horrible sin, which however strong the temptation, must be avoided. He consequently reverted to his former habit, and for years afterwards viewed it not as an evil but as a positive good, since it was a means to him of avoiding the sin of fornication. "O!" wrote he, "that my father, or some one else, had conversed with me on matters of this kind at this period, it would have prevented all this suffering. But no; all such subjects were prohibited from being mentioned, and I went on sinning against God, and against my own constitution, in complete ignorance." He went on to say that about two years after he had thus commenced this deadly habit, he began to look pale and emaciated, his appetite fell off, he experienced severe pains in the back part of the head, and in the testes and loins, seminal emissions frequently occurred, and he was fast becoming the shadow of his former self. His friends began to be alarmed at his appearance, the family medical man was consulted; his lungs were examined and declared sound, and the disease pronounced general debility, which a change of air and tonic medicines would probably remove. The tonic medicines, in the shape of large doses of quinine, were administered; the sea coast was resorted to for change of air, but he experienced no relief. The root of the disease had escaped attention, and, as a matter of course, the symptoms did not improve. At this period the patient himself had not the slightest idea that the debilitated state of his frame originated in the habit he had been so long practising. He thus continued to grow worse and worse, and his friends made up their minds that whatever might be the cause of his disease he certainly would never recover. Celebrated physicians were now consulted, but the habit that was draining the fountains of the body of their vitality was never referred to, and the consequence was that the treatment had no effect. At length the young man began to notice a great change in his genital organs; the scrotum hung down in the pendulous state before mentioned; on the left side no testicle could be felt, but in its place a number of hard cords; there was an apparent diminution in size of the external parts, and an eruption made its appearance under the prepuce. It was whilst in this state that in the course of his reading he came across the " Confessions of Jean Jacques Rousseau,' which completely opened his eyes, and he now saw clearly the nature of the horrible vice he had for so many years indulged in, and the consequences which were now, in misery to himself, flowing from it.

I had considerable difficulty with this case, on account of the extent to which the mischief had proceeded; but as he had a naturally strong constitution, and the revulsion of feeling consequent on suddenly learning the nature of the vice in which he had been indulging gave him sufficient strength of resolution to conquer it, and to persevere in the treatment I employed, the result was completely successful.

This case alone should be sufficient to shew the evil of keeping youth in ignorance of the nature of the generative organs, and the consequences of their abuse.

Impotence declares itself with great rapidity in persons who are addicted to masturbation, especially when exposed to influences calculated to injure health. The testes, as already mentioned, rapidly become flaccid and shrivelled. The distressing sense of weight, so frequently described as a dragging pain, further tends to prove the organic changes going on in these organs; the muscular fibres, which were described when speaking of the anatomy of the parts, lose their contractility, which they never do in a healthy condition, hence the symptoms described.

The phenomena which attend the various forms of sexual debility create much difficulty in the attempt to represent them.

An individual thus afflicted after a while presents a melancholy and dejected appearance. He is restless, ever and again desiring a change, but disinclined to physical exercise. He seeks solitude, and by allowing his thoughts to dwell on the fact of his disability, frequently becomes hypochondriacal. In business he loses self-confidence, and is constantly in dread of some unforseen event about to happen to him. His temper likewise becomes irritable, and he is the subject of most sudden exacerbations of anger and passion. Muscular debility, characterised by fatigue, lassitude, and pain in the loins on the slightest exertion, prevails to a most distressing degree. The healthy colour of the skin disappears, the eyes lose their brightness, and are surrounded by a dark halo, while the state of the digestive organs becomes exceedingly distressing. But it is the immediate effect of an over-excited state of the generative organs to lower the vital energy of the system; the consequence is, that great organic and constitutional disturbance ensues.

The functions of the brain are the earliest to declare the secret fact; giddiness and headache are more or less present; memory becomes defective, and the power of commanding and controlling the ideas is lost, while a frequent disinclination to enjoy the usual amount of sleep terminates in general and extreme physical exhaustion.

It is my firm opinion that abuse of the sexual feelings is the frequent cause of mental derangement; the primary cause of the complaint being but too often entirely ignored in ordinary treatment, and the subsequent symptoms treated as if the brain had been the organ primarily affected.*

There appears but little doubt that the morbid state of the nervous system, more particularly the spinal cord, which is produced by excessive sexual intercourse, is analagous to that which is sometimes observed in the muscles after excessive exercise. And it seems a fair analogy which suggests that the loss of nervous power, and especially the paraplegia, that may follow long-continued sexual excess, are due to changes very similar to those that are witnessed in the progressive muscular atrophy after great muscular exertion; the softening and wasting of the spinal cord being a process of degeneration essentially similar to that traced in the muscles.

It must never be forgotten that seminal emission is associated with what may be regarded as violent exercise of the spinal cord.

It is, besides, the peculiar character of seminiferous losses, but more especially when self-provoked, to establish an order of symptoms which appear to have their seat in the region of the stomach; the epigastrium become tender

* Since writing the above I find that Dr. Ritchie, resident physician of Bethnal House Asylum, in a paper published in the *Lancet* of February 16, entitled "An Enquiry into a frequent cause of Insanity in Young Men," states, as regards "the frequency of cases of insanity arising from masturbation," that in that asylum in a per-centage from that cause was, in the private class, 1 in 7·98, and in the pauper class 1 in 16·16; and referring to the possibility of its being thought that that proportion was exaggerated or overstated, says, "Would it were so!"

to the touch; a sensation of faintness referred to this spot is complained of; also occasional pain, flatulence, a sense of distension, and other anomalous symptoms.

These symptoms are undoubtedly the result of venereal excitement, implicating the central ganglia of the sympathetic nervous system.

Hence we have the strongest reason to infer, that when undue excitement of the generative functions causes irritation of these ganglia, this undue excitement will be thus communicated to the spinal cord, producing depression of spirits, pain at the pit of the stomach, and general prostration.

If such be the nature of these complicated nervous phenomena, it is notaltogether so surprising as it would otherwise be, that in the worst cases which occur of excesses in young men, nature has been sometimes unable to recover from too rapidly repeated shocks.

The irritation thus set up has morbidly excited the channels of nervous influence, producing in them some permanent injury, from which they never wholly recover.

It is also a similar sympathetic influence thus morbidly developed that re-acts on the kidneys as well as the stomach, causing them to pour out a considerable quantity of thick, muddy, unhealthy urine; and an irritability of the bladder, inducing a frequent desire to micturate.

Many of the foregoing symptoms were apparent in case 1563, which I treated successfully by correspondence only. The patient thus writes:

"At the age of about fifteen I acquired the fearful habit of masturbation, and continued an ignorant devotee and victim of it until I was twenty-one (nine months ago). By accident I became acquainted with the terrible effects of this habit last winter; but though I tried hard, and prayed earnestly for strength to free myself from its shackles, I was not enabled to do so thoroughly till about the middle of April last, when I discovered the havoc it was commiting on my frame. I then appeared like one for the gráve. Unfortunately I applied to an advertised doctor, who sent me an instrument for comprossing the penis,* accompanied with certain prescriptions; but the instrument caused such violent and painful eroctions that I was compelled to discontinue the use of it. I then thought I could do without medical treatment, if I lived according to a prescribed diet, and took plenty of exercise: Nature, thought I, will repair the loss. Still I cannot disguise from myself that I am gradually getting thinner and weaker. I have not yet lost the power of erecting the penis; and although, previously to the use of the above-mentioned instrument, I never involuntarily had an erection for days together—not even when my imagination was excited by wicked thoughts, it now happens almost everymorning, and at times I feel strongly tempted to commence the old habit again; but

* This is not the only instance in which this clumsy and mischievous treatment had been previously adopted by patients who have consulted me. It is about as reasonable as would be an attempt to stop an inclination to vomit by compressing the throat.

then a shudder passes over me, and I conquer the inclination. Sometimes my eyes appear of a muddy cast, which causes me to feel very uneasy : but in a day or two they get clearer again, and hope is again in the ascendant. I frequently have a dull pain in the region of the spine, but that which causes me the greatest apprehension is the remarkable dreams I have at night. At one time I am engaged in eager dispute with some one, in which the passions of anger, fear, joy, &c., are alternately predominant ; at another time I seem engaged in the greatest physical exertion, such as running, fighting, or lifting some tremendous weight ; these all tend to fatigue my body, and deprive it of its due amount of rest. The daily routine of my avocation also fatigues me much more than it was wont ; and my memory is unquestionably impaired. I forgot to say that a pain in the region of the left kidney sometimes attacks me, and on such occasions the urine appears very muddy ; and although my testicles are not in such a pendulous state as they were three months since, I can feel that a small lump appears to be forming under both. I fear that my symptoms are those of an early stage of consumption."

It must be borne in mind, also, that masturbation determines a specific and important change in the prostatic portion of the urethra—a knowledge of which is of great importance in reference to treatment.

As it is impossible to trace the effects of masturbation or venereal excesses into anything like detail, I present to the notice of my readers the result of the researches of eminent physiologists, showing the whole material development of the human body, in reference to its average weight at different periods of life, which will afford us some valuable general information, and also precise data, to enable us to judge of the ill effects which venereal excesses of any kind are likely to occasion at different ages :—

				lbs.	ozs.
At	1	year the body weighs	. .	21	0
"	5	"	" . .	35	0
"	10	"	" . .	54	0
"	12	"	" . .	64	14
"	15	"	" . .	95	8
"	20	"	" . .	132	0
"	25	"	" . .	138	0
"	40	"	(the maximum)	139	0½

The preceding table proves approximately that man only reaches the maximum of his weight at the age of forty, whilst the increase from twenty-five is hardly perceptible. It may therefore be safely inferred than the human economy reaches its full vigour at that age. When we reflect that masturbation is chiefly indulged in by persons from twelve to twenty, or even twenty-five years of age, we may readily conceive the evil it is likely to cause, as, at the age of twelve, when that vice has but too frequently become a habit of some duration, the individual would have still to gain about sixty per cent. of his weight.

His growth, although nearly finished at the age of twenty-five, will not be completely so, since even after thirty the weight of the body is susceptible of an almost imperceptible increase. Now, when we consider that masturbation and youthful lust is pursued with reckless indifference at a time—as we see from preceding data—when all the energies of the body are required for its sustenation and growth; I ask with all earnestness what room is there to doubt the ill consequences which must result from premature and excessive indulgence in venereal pleasures.

I cannot do better than close this chapter with a self-drawn picture by a patient, at that time in one of the healthiest parts of South America, whom I had the good fortune to succeed in restoring to perfect health.

After mentioning his position, &c., and that he was induced to apply to me by the accident of one of my books falling into his hands, he goes on to say, "For the last twelve years I have practised the degrading vice of self-abuse, or masturbation, without being aware of its fearful results, and which first commenced as the result of a lascivious dream without any incitement on my part, and the pleasure then experienced has been the cause of its continuance; and though I have several times endeavoured to break it off as a filthy habit, have never succeeded. I have never cohabited with any of the other sex, though the desire was almost irresistible a few years since. But thanks to the

good precepts of virtuous parents, I have never
committed myself. I have been subject for the
last two years to nocturnal emissions, the result
of lascivious dreams after being in ladies' company; the emissions are unattended with pleasure, without erection of the penis, and are of a
thin, watery nature; the penis hangs down in a
pendulous state, is very diminutive in size, as
are all the external parts, but has not wholly
lost the power of erection. I am terriby afraid
I am suffering from spermatorrhœa, as I have
noticed three or four times, while making water
in the daytime, a small quantity of thin white
matter escapes with the last few drops, and upon
passing urine into a phial, observe after a few
hours, towards the bottom, a transparent filmy
substance, which floats upon the least agitation.
I see you request some urine for examination,
but I know of no available means of sending
any, and trust you can judge without. My
constitution is undermined, my mental powers
are much impaired; I have lost all bodily
strength, and have little or no appetite, am pale,
thin, and emaciated, most dreadfully nervous,
subject to fits of melancholy, and rendered
morose in disposition. My water is short and
rather high coloured during the day, which,
right or wrong; I have attributed to rheumatics,
as the least exertion makes me perspire profusely;
consequently I take cold easily, and experience a
dull pain in the loins, about the kindneys, which

the doctors tell me is rheumatics. I have been under their treatment for some years as a sufferer from general debility. I have been subject of late to a slight disfiguration in the forehead, in the shape of a number of small red pimples which I cannot get rid of. I suffer a good deal from dyspepsia, though I am temperate in my diet, and seldom drink wine or spirits ; I also suffer a good deal from constipation of the bowels. And now, Doctor, you will say my case is a serious one: I know it ; and the fact of being engaged to an amiable and accomplished young lady whom I had known several years, coupled with the terrible, fearful thoughts of impotency, drives me almost wild. As a Christian, and one who I believe has the welfare of his fellow men at heart, I beseech you to do what you can to restore some of my former vigour; I must tell you, since my eyes have been opened by the perusal of your work, I have given up, and for ever, the vile practice that has been draining away my life's blood. God grant it may (through your help) not be too late."

———

In the commencing part of the foregoing extract it is mentioned that "*Spermatorrhœa*" (the worst, perhaps, of the effects of self-pollution) has a chapter specially devoted to it. I have deemed it expedient, in consequence of the difficulty of making any subdivision in it, to introduce that chapter (Chap. VI.) in its entirety.

SPERMATORRHŒA.

———

The term spermatorrhœa is applied in all cases where emissions of seminal fluid take place otherwise than in obedience to the impulse arising from the natural act of coition, or the will of the person in whom it occurs.

It has been already remarked* that the seminal fluid is stored up in the vesiculæ seminales, and that small ducts open from the junction of these with the vasa deferentia into the urethra, and that, by means of these ducts, the fluid escapes. Now, in the healthy state, these ducts are continually kept closed, so that the semen cannot escape, except in obedience to the impulse arising from the natural act of coition; but when they become weakened by excessive venery, or, what is more common, by the habit to which the last chapter was devoted, dilatation follows, and the slightest degree of pressure will cause the semen —as yet imperfectly formed—to escape; such pressure, for example, as would be present when the fæces were passing through the rectum, or when the bladder was contracting to empty

* This refers to the work on the " Philosophy of Marriage," not to this Catalogue, and the reader who wishes to understand this description thoroughly, must refer to the work itself.

itself. It will be remembered that the vesiculæ seminales are situated immediately between the bladder and the rectum, so that, when the fœces are passing down the latter, there is necessarily pressure upon the vesicles, and, consequently, it is then that the first symptoms of spermatorrhœa may be observed. The same thing occurs when the bladder is contracting to expel the urine, and for a similar reason; a quantity of thick slimy fluid may be observed passing with the last few drops, which, upon examination, most frequently proves to be semen. Should the weakness, and, consequently, the dilitation continue to increase, it will require no pressure to force away the seminal fluid, for it will escape as it arrives from the vas deferens, not remaining in the vesicles, but passing immediately into the urethra, either making its exit thereby, or passing backwards into the bladder, and mingling with the urine.

The disease called spermatorrhœa is one of the most common results of masturbation; indeed it is almost an invariable result, for it is next to an impossibility for any person to practice this baneful habit for any length of time, without suffering from the involuntary escape of seminal fluid, either with the urine or otherwise. It does not follow, however, that if an individual suffers from emissions, that, therefore, he must have been guilty of the vice of Onanism. The disease may have had its origin in excessive venery, or weakness from other causes, and in s. me cases I have no doubt it is constitutional. "The vesiculæ seminales," says Lallemand, "take on the habit of contracting themselves under the influence of excitement less energetic than usual, and quite abnormally so. In such cases, a full bladder or rectum, a bed too warm or too soft, lying on the back, warm or exciting drinks, &c. provoke emissions more readily than they ought. It is in such instances that the intimate and reciprocal connection between the vesiculæ seminales and the brain produces lacivious dreams, *le plus deser-donnes*, under the slightest direct or indirect excitement of the genital organs and inevitable pollutions, from the reproduction of all the ideas which are connected with those of generation" Among the common causes of spermatorrhœa, I might place hæmorrhoids (piles) a long foreskin, accumulation of foreign matter with the secretion under the prepuce, drinking large quantities of alcoholic drinks. gonorrhœa, venereal excess, and even, though it may seem paradoxical, excessive continence : but the most common of all is weakness of the genital urinary apparatus, resulting from the habit before named.

Sometimes the disease makes its appearance long after the habit itself has been abandoned, but when adequate exciting causes suddenly reveal the mischief which has been entailed upon the system. Such cases, if immediately attended to and properly treated, are capable of speedy cure.

93

Thus, in case 1043* the patient, a young man of twenty-four years of age, informed me that he had practised masturbation whilst at school, but had left it off for nearly ten years, and had recently had sexual intercourse with females, much more frequently than he thought, to use his own words, "did him good;" for the preceding week he had felt a little pain in the penis, and had noticed on going to stool, a quantity of white glutinous matter pass away from the urethra. I requested him to furnish me with some of the matter on a piece of glass, which he did, and on examining it by the microscope, I detected spermatozon; I ordered a lotion to be applied to the genital organs morning and evening, and medicine to be taken internally; and in three weeks both the pain and the discharge had disappeared.

In the healthy condition of the generative organs, the seminal fluid is continually being formed, and stored up in the vesiculæ seminales, to be either re-absorbed or ejected from the system at regular intervals; but the formation of this fluid, like that of most other secretions, is very much under the control of the nervous system, and will consequently be much increased by the mind being continually directed towards objects calculated to excite the sexual propensity; and thus if it be frequently ejected, a much larger

* The numbers mentioned in this and other cases quoted in this work are merely references to my Case Book

quantity will be produced, at a terrible expense to the other organs of the body. When, therefore, a morbid condition of those organs has been brought about by excessive venery, or any other evil habit, so as to give rise to spermatorrhœa. and the patient suffers from the continual escape of this vital fluid, the quantity that may be secreted and passed away is absolutely alarming to any one who understands the physiology of the human body.

One form, and a very common one, in which we meet with spermatorrhœa, is the escape of seminal fluid during the night, accompanied with erection of the penis, and erotic and lascivious dreams; the emission in this case is generally supposed to arise from the excitement of the pictures produced by the imagination; this is, however, by no means the case. "The general belief," says Lalleland, "exists that erotic dreams produce nocturnal pollutions, and they are looked upon as very dangerous; but lascivious pictures, which occur during sleep, arise from excitement of the genital organs, just as erections and spasmodic contraction of the vesiculœ seminales do; all these phenomena coincide, because they depend upon one and the same cause, but the one does not depend upon the other."

In case 547, a young man of a nervous and excitable temperament wrote to me that he had practised masturbation for many years, in fact, had commenced it as early as he could remember and had continued it till within a few months of the time he wrote, at which period his age was twenty-one. For the year preceding he had suffered from emissions, but in a trifling degree —as he called it—once a week or sometimes a little oftener. More recently, however, he had never slept a night without having his rest interrupted by dreams of a most lascivious character, which dreams always ended with his consummating his wishes as he imagined, by which the morning revealed to him as copious emissions, his night clothes and the bed being wet with the fluid which had escaped. As this was rather a serious case, a personal interview was demanded. This request complied with, I found as I had anticipated, varicocele in one testicle, and the whole of the genital organs in a state of great irritation. I prescribed Elixir Mynsichti, * and Mur Aur. et Sod. (a preparation of gold), with a good result, and by subsequent treatment had the satisfaction of effecting a perfect restoration to health.

This is a very common form of spermatorrhœa. Scarcely a day passes without my seeing patients whose symptoms are analagous to those I have just detailed. The disease, like an assassin, attacks its victim during sleep, and when, consequently he has no power to ward off the blow. Even on those nights when emissions do not occur, still the patient suffers from gloomy and terrible fancies breaking in upon his slumbers, haunting his imagination, and reviving any in-

* This and many other remedies mentioned in my works are not to be found in the English Pharmacopœia

cidents of an unpleasant nature which have occurred during the day.

Sometimes the escape of seminal fluid is experienced at regular intervals during the day apparently without any direct cause. The patient may be walking, or sitting in one position or another, when he suddenly feels a quantity of fluid escaping from the urethra, without exciting any pleasurable sensation, and in the entire absence of erection of the penis.

In case 2162 the patient stated that a few days before he had attempted intercourse with his wife, and had failed; at first there was an erection, which, however, soon subsided, without any escape of semen, and then all sexual power was gone. He had been many years in India, and had enjoyed very good health, but for the preceding three or four weeks had suffered from the escape of what he supposed to be semen, which had passed away generally whilst taking a lounge on the sofa, and smoking his pipe after dinner. This was not the result of an erection, nor did it occasion any pleasurable sensation. He had, he stated, practised Onanism during his youth, but did not think it was that, or he should have felt the ill-effects of it before. I ordered cold bathing every morning, and prescribed Bromuret of Potass, Balsam Vitæ Hoffmani, Electuar, aromatic, and during convalescence, Aq. Carminatio Regia; and the patient was gradually restored to health and manly vigour.

The worst from of spermatorrhœa, because the

one most likely to escape detection is that where the semen escapes by the ducts into the urethra, not, however, to be immediately ejected from the system, but to pass backward into the bladder, and then to be brought away with the urine. In this way the disease may go on for years without even being suspected; and the person who finds himself, from this cause, suffering from general debility and nervousness, wonders what can have given rise to the symptoms under which he labors.

In case 931, the patient consulted me, to know if I could point out any probable cause why his wife had not borne children. He stated that he had been married four years, had lived rather freely previously, but did not think he suffered any ill-effects from it, as he was able to have intercourse with his wife, although he admitted that the pleasure experienced during the injection of semen was not as great as formerly. Thinking he might suffer from this form of spermatorrhœa, I requested him to bring me some of his urine, which he did. Upon examination it was found to contain large numbers of spermatozoa, but not perfect ones; most of them with the tails broken off, or mutilated in some other way. I therefore informed him that the cause of his wife's barrenness was obvious, the seminal fluid being of such a character as could not possibly fecundate an ovum. Under the treatment I adopted, viz., great moderation in indulgence of sexual congress, cold douches against the spinal column, and the administration of Osmund regal, &c., his seminal fluid was restored to its normal condition.

The broken or imperfect form of spermatozoa (Fig. V.) is a common consequence of spermatorrhœa, and is frequently met with in that disease.

Fig. V.

Occasionally very peculiar cases occur, in which all the usual symptoms are absent, as illustrated by case 1432, in which the consultation took place by correspondence only.

The patient wrote me that he was a strong, vigorous, muscular man, aged twenty-four, six feet in stature, and weighing fifteen stone. He stated that he had an excellent appetite, the best of spirits, was not at all nervous, did not suffer from any of the symptoms indicative of seminal discharges mentioned in a previous work of mine, the perusal of which had induced nim to consult me, but was nevertheless impotent. He went on to say—"I have consulted medical men; they laugh at me, and tell me it is imagination. But I am the last man in the world to imagine myself into a disease. From my appearance they all admit this, but offer no other explanation. Tell me, have you ever seen a case like mine, and can afford me any relief?"

I wrote to inform him that his case was by no means so uncommon as he appeared to suppose. He accordingly placed himself under my care, and, after a proper course of treatment, manhood was restored.

In reference to spermatorrhœa, there are two

points of the greatest possible importance, on
which I feel it imperative to make a few remarks;
and these are, *firstly*, the mode of detecting spermatorrhœa, *i, e.*, its diagnosis, and, *secondly*, the
treatment to be adopted. In reference to the first
point, there can be no difficulty where the semen
escapes in large quantities during the day, either
from excitement or otherwise; nor is the difficulty
great when it assumes the form of nocturnal
emissions, because, generally, the patient will be
aware when it is passing, and if not, will observe
in the morning that his linen, or the bedclothes,
will be wet or stained; but the most common
form of this disease, as I have already remarked,
is that wherein the seminal fluid escapes with the
urine, and here the difficulty will be very great.
The patient will not be aware of any emission
taking place, and the medical man can only make
the discovery after the most difficult investiga-
tions. Prior to the discovery of the spermatozoa
in the semen, the detection of spermatorrhœa
was altogether beyond the reach of the most
distinguished pathologist.

At that time, if a patient, who was suffering
from atrophy, or wasting away, and general debility of the whole system, presented himself to
a physician, the first impression of the latter
would be that the lungs or heart were affected;
on examining these organs, however, he might
probably ascertain them to be sound. The glands
of the mesentery might then be suspected of
disease. The suspicion discovered to be ground-
less, the patient would then be interrogated as
to whether he suffered from emissions, to which

he would reply, not to his knowledge. Other examinations would then be made, and with the same want of success. A great obscurity would thus rest over the diagnosis, and the utmost that could occur would be to *suspect* the escape of semen with the urine. Probably this suspicion would not have arisen, and even if it had would have been *but* a suspicion. These remarks will apply with equal force to other diseases resulting from spermatorrhœa, as well as general debility. The following case will serve as a good illustration. It is the case (copied from the *Medical and Physical Journal*) of a patient who was treated by Sir Benjamin Brodie, in St. George's Hospital. "The patient was admitted into the hospital on account of a pain in the left testicle. The organ was soft, flaccid, and about a third of the size of the opposite one. The patient had not received any injury, nor had he had gonorrhœa, but for five years had practised masturbation once a day. The testicle, before it had wasted, was the seat of a very severe pain and swelling. The patient was sad and melancholy. Various remedies were tried in vain and he left the hospital without relief."

Now, who that has seen anything of spermatorrhœa can doubt that the patient suffered from emission of semen with the urine? I had recently under my treatment a case very similar to the one just described, wherein a microscopic investigation of the urine demonstrated the presence of spermatozoa.

And I must here digress for a moment, to say

a word or two respecting that noblest instrument
of natural philosophy, the miscroscope.

In contemplating the swarms of living atoms
which teem " in the leaves of every forest ; in the
flowers of every garden, and in the waters of
every rivulet," when placed in the field of a
powerful microscope, the idea which most strongly
impresses the mind after the first sensation of
surprise has subsided is the infinitesimal minute-
ness and simple form of many of the structures
in which that marvellous principle, LIFE, is en-
shrined. We have been accustomed to associate
the presence of vitality with bodies possessing
various complicated organs for the elaboration
and maintenance of the energies of existence ; but
here we see perfect and distinct creatures, in the
condition of simple globules and cells, that " live
and move and have their being," and increase in
numbers with a rapidity so prodigious, and in
modes so peculiar, as to startle all our precon-
ceived notions of animal organisation.

It is by a profound investigation of the modifl-
cations of structure and functions exhibited in
these minute organisms, that so much light has
been thrown upon what were previously some
of the most obscure phenomena in human
physiology.

It was by the microscope that the existence of
spermatozoa was revealed to us ; until then, that
distinction which we pointed out in describing
the various secretions of the different parts of the
generative organism was altogether unknown
and unsuspected. Once known, however, it not

only threw a flood of light upon physiological science, but upon pathology also; for the same instrument which revealed to us the *normal* in physiology, also enables us to examine the *abnormal*.

It must not be supposed, however, that the microscope is an instrument which it is as easy to use as a common magnifying glass—far from it: its efficient use for scientific purposes, especially pathological ones, requires unwearied patience, long practice, and acute powers of observation. As Captain Basil Hall observes in speaking of a kindred instrument, "The secret often lies in knowing exactly what to look for, and thence learning how to adjust, not merely the focus of the eye, but what may be termed the focus of the judgment; so as to be able to pitch the understanding into such a key that the information may be understood when it comes."

Returning, however, to the subject matter of this chapter, it will be perceived, that the discovery, by the microscope, of spermatozoa in the semen, was not only most valuable in a philosophic point of view, but much more so as a matter of diagnosis. It enabled us to detect the most difficult diseases that we had to deal with, and exposed to noon-day view matters which before lay hid in the darkness of an Egyptian night.

But notwithstanding this, the spermatozoa are not to be discovered as readily as might be imagined, even with the greatest skill, care, and experience on the part of the physician. The urine may probably be examined three or four times, and no spermatozoa be present; but the next time they may be discovered. The semen, too, when it has escaped into the bladder, is generally found mixed with urinary deposits, such as lithic acid, lithate of ammonia, oxalate of lime, epithelium, mucus, &c., and there is great difficulty in distinguishing the spermatozoa amidst all these deposits; and it must also be remembered that we rarely meet with the spermatozoa in their perfect condition. In nine cases out of ten they are in the broken, mutilated condition before referred to. Hence it requires a good amount of careful examination to be able to diagnose successfully in these cases.

In case 3250 the patient stated that he suffered from great debility, which; in fact, was evident enough from his appearance. He had been under the treatment of several physicians, and every one had declared, after a microscopic examination of the urine, that semen was not present. As he informed me that he had when at college, practised masturbation, I felt convinced that I should detect spermatozoa, notwithstanding what those he had previously consulted might have said to the contrary. I examined the urine, and had great difficulty in telling what was present, in consequence of the large quantity of urinary deposits which obstructed the view. On the first occasion, although the examination occupied an hour, I could detect no semen. Still, however unsatisfied, I made another examination three or four days later, and after great difficulty detected spermatozoa, but excessively mutilated and broken to pieces. The cause of the debility now made out, the method of treatment, of course, became evident.

The tendency to the frequent occurrence of involuntary seminal emissions is always more or less increased by an attack of gonorrhœa. A diminution of the involuntary discharges may, and usually does, follow the cure of gonorrhœa; but this must not be taken for a proof of the restoration of the general apparatus to a normal condition. The slightest cause of irritation is sufficient to re-establish the disease with increased severity. Sometimes this apparent change of symptoms indicates that the case is lapsing into one of confirmed impotency.

The following case, 2534, is a very instructive one. It cannot be better described than in the patient's own language in his first letter. He says:—"It is with a deep sense of shame and self-condemnation that I address you, being in a fearful state of ill-health, brought about, as I believe, principally by that filthy practice which you so truly denominate self-pollution. I am now about twenty years of age, and acquired the habit I have named about six years ago, when at school, and continued it for about four or five years, when experiencing sudden pains in the loins, and frequently observing a gummy, sticky oily fluid oozing from the penis, especially in the morning, sometimes only slightly, and just glueing together the lips of the opening, but at other times more copiously, I became alarmed, and applied to a person in London, and took his medicines for a considerable time, but without the slightest benefit. I unfortunately, too, contracted gonorrhœa, which was cured with copaiba, &c.; and for some little time afterwards, although I felt excessively weak, the gluey fluid, which had increased during the gonorrhœa, became gradually diminished. I left England about that time, hoping that nature and my new occupations and change of scene and air, would restore me to health; but I soon became worse than ever, so much so that I was obliged to return to London. I then consulted another medical man, who told me that my gonorrhœa had been imperfectly cured, and he again gave me copaiba; and I assure you the quantities of that remedy I have swallowed, either alone or in combination with other drugs, is almost incredible. Finding no relief, I have at last given it up in despair and disgust, and now write to you in the hope that you may be able to restore me to health and vigour. I am not now in London, as you see by the heading of this letter, and therefore cannot at present consult you personally; but I will briefly describe my present symptoms. What I suffer most from, and what I feel is gradually draining life and strength away from me, is the emission of semen, especially after taking a few glasses of wine, or being in the company of ladies, or any excitement otherwise occasioned. My testicles are in a very pendulous state, and are getting smaller and smaller every day, especially the left one, which seems to be a lot of hard cords. My face and parts of the body are covered with pimples and the slightest degree of fatigue utterly exhausts me. I also feel at times a dull sense of pain, which I cannot describe, along the penis, extending to its furthermost parts, and the urine is very different in appearance to what I fancy it should be. I feel quite certain that unless I obtain speedy relief I shall soon be in my grave: for besides the bodily symptoms, I find myself labouring under such despondency of mind, that, conjointly, I am sure my system cannot long hold out against them. I send you, by same mail as this, a small bottle containing some of my urine, and also a portion of the discharge between two pieces of clean glass."

This case is remarkably illustrative of the mischief arising from a mistaken diagnosis—spermatorrhœa having been erroneously taken for gonorrhœa; and I doubt not that oceans of cepaiba, &c., are administered prejudicially in hundreds of similar cases; and it demonstrates, also, the importance of microscopic examination of urine, &c., in such cases, as I had no difficulty in at once obtaining proof that the impression I had formed upon reading his letter, viz., that he was suffering from a severe form of spermatorrhœa, was well founded.

The treatment of spermatorrhœa is, like the diagnosis, exceedingly difficult, and requires, also, much skill and experience. The disease arises, as has been shown, from a variety of causes, and each, as a matter of course, will require treatment peculiar to itself. Lallemand, having observed the benefit that followed the application of nitrate of silver, or as it is commonly called, lunar caustic to the eye, when its vessels were relaxed by disease, inferred that the application of the same substance to the seminal ducts, when they were relaxed, would be productive of equal benefit. He, therefore, invented an instrument for this purpose, called the *porte castique* : and hence arose one of the most brutal modes of treating an affection, with which the whole range of medical science can furnish us. Even supposing this application of caustic to be valuable, which I dispute—and admitting the possibility . of the operator being quite certain when he has reached the ducts, and therefore, knowing when to cauterize, which I deny—still the application of so destructive an agent to such a delicate part as the membrane lining the urethra, cannot but be productive of the worst results. How many hundreds of cases of stricture can be traced to this horrible treatment. How many persons have had to curse the day that English practitioners adopted this French mode of treating spermatorrhœa, or that on which they were foolish enough to submit themselves to it.

The employment of the solid nitrate of silver as a remedy in spermatorrhœa, is not only dangerous, but it implies a total disregard of the true pathology of that disease.

The objections to the application of the solid caustic to the urethra, are the intense pain with which its use is attended—the risk of retention of urine following the application—the well-known liability of caustic to occasion severe attacks of rigor—the danger of profuse urethra hemorrhage, arising on the separation of the slough which its application must produce ; and, lastly, the danger that the sloughing process may involve the membranes of the urinary canal to such an extent as to destroy its integrity, and thereby expose the patient to all the sufferings and dangers resulting from infiltration of urine, fistula, and the like.

It is allowed by all unprejudiced persons that the result of actual experience far outweigh the most spacious theories, or the boldest assertions. I therefore select a few cases out of many that have come under my notice, in which the effects of cauterization of the prostatic and other portions of the urethra proved most serious and distressing.

In case 1742, the patient had led a most dissolute life, and suffered at various times from repeated attacks of gonorrhœa; the consequence, at last, being that he suffered from obstinate urethral and vesicular gleet and a shattered constitution. He applied for surgical aid, when cauterization was recommended and applied, the effects of which the patient described as terrible in the extreme—the scalding on micturating was for nearly three days beyond description, the difficulty being such as almost to amount to retention. A purulent discharge ensued, tinged with blood, which continued for several days. On recovery from the local effects of the caustic, the posterior part of the urethra became the seat of a severe and fixed pain, always intensified by the escape of urine. Sexual intercourse, attempted on several occasions, created so much pain and inconvenience that it was abandoned. Nocturnal emissions were of frequent occurrence, and also discharge from the vesiculæ seminales, whenever defæcation took place. In this condition he consulted me. On attempting to pass a bougie along the anterior part of the urethra much pain was complained of; but when it reached the posterior part, it was excruciating, and the spasms so violent, that it had to be withdrawn. Two or three days being allowed to elapse and, in the meantime, sedative and efficient medicine administered, another attempt was made with a smaller-sized bougie, which entered the bladder, but not without much pain and difficulty.

This clearly showed that permanent stricture was most imminent. I obviated this, however, by catheterising the urethra ; and at the same time successfully counteracted other local and general symptoms by a suitable course of medicines.

Case 1715 came under my care many months subsequent to cauterization. The patient was a gentleman, evidently of a highly nervous temperament ; but since the local action of the caustic, the pain of the urethra had never finally left him, and there was also great irritation of the canal. His description of the immediate results of the action of the solid caustic was truly appalling. To be brief, great mischief resulted to the patient ; so much so that he became the victim of a settled melancholy. Similar treatment was pursued in

D

this case to combat the local disease, which resulted in considerable relief; but after a period of seven weeks, I deemed it advisable to order him on a tour, as it was evident that time and change alone would alter the state of the mental feelings': and this with the accompanying remedial treatment, gradually eradicated the ill-effects caused by the injudicious use of the caustic.

The cases will suffice to show that not only does no permanent benefit attend the local action of the solid caustic, but that by its use an array of symptoms become developed, which in some cases bid defiance to every treatment which ingenuity and skill can suggest.

Nor am I alone in the opinions I have expressed on this matter, for a celebrated author says of Lallemand (after having spoken of the services which he had rendered to suffering humanity):—"He has, however, by an exaggerated representation of the effect of cauterization in curing spermatorrhœa, not only impaired the value of his contributions to science, but likewise injured the patients themselves; inasmuch as by reading his book, they have been thrown into a disconsolate state about the future, almost amounting to despair, when the vaunted infallible remedy of cauterization has not immediately produced the promised effect."

The daily introduction of bougies is also to be condemned, several cases having come under my notice in which the previous reckless use of that instrument gave rise to symptoms of a most dangerous character.

This remark does not apply to an occasional use of the bougie in suitable cases; on the contrary, I have found in many instances that an irritable urethra, with tendency to stricture, has been completely cured after a few applications.

The treatment of the various phases of spermatorrhœa, and of the diseases known under the generic term—debility, require, perhaps, more skill and experience than any other derangements to which the physicial organization is subject. These are affections in which the treatment must not be limited to the remedies employed in the practice of one country, or contained in the Pharmacopœia of another. The cases are sometimes so desperate, and the remedies required so potent, that all lands must be ransacked for the latter. We must not confine ourselves to the vegetable kingdom; nor seek to obtain antidotes exclusively from the animal or mineral; nature in her totality must be searched for remedial agents.

Now this is not done by the major part of those who treat these diseases. They are content with the ordinary routine of treatment, no matter how often it has been weighed in the balance and found wanting, and the result is that which would be expected—the disorders are very rarely cured. Indeed, how English practitioners can with their limited Pharmacopœia treat affections of this kind, except in early and simple cases, is to me a mystery. They are really, strictly speaking, no remedies in the English Pharmacopœia which can be relied on in these and other disorders of the generative organism. If the question be asked, what can be employed successfully for the purpose of thoroughly eradicating syphillis from the system? and what to restore the system to health in the debility occasioned by self-abuse? or what to stop the spermatorrhœa, the cause of that debility? the answer, doubtless, is ready — mercury for the former, tonics for the latter. To which I reply—In the first place, I dispute that mercury will have any such effect; and, secondly, if it had, it would only be at the expense of the future health; and as to the tonics—more particularly the ordinary tonics of English practice —these will have no such result; they cannot stop the escape of semen in a bad case of spermatorrhœa. The following case, 2489, may serve as an illustration.

The patient stated that he had for years been afflicted with nocturnal emissions, and that for the previous few months he had been totally unable to cohabit with his wife. He had consulted many medical men, but without any beneficial result. He had taken quinine, iron, and the vegetable bitters in surprising quantities: in fact, he thought he had taken everything in the list of the Materia Medica, and consequently he completely despaired of ever being cured. As a last resource, however, he came to me. I supplied him with a mixture and lotion, which I usually employ in cases of a character analogous to his. On taking the bottles into his hand I observed a smile pass over his countenance, and on inquiring the cause, he remarked that he fancied his system was already impregnated pretty strongly with what I had given him, as he had taken everything. I replied that I was quite sure

he had neither taken the mixture or employed the
lotion that I gave him. He seemed doubtful, and
I offered to convince him, by writing a prescription containing the drugs I had employed, and
allowing him to get it made up at any druggist's
he might select. I took this course for the
double purpose of convincing him that my
medicines were neither employed by English
medical men, nor to be obtained in this country,
and also to show him that, notwithstanding that
fact, I did not wish to pretend to give secret
remedies. The prescription was as follows:

  ℞
   Elixir Acid. Haller, ℥ss
   Aqua Laurocerasi ℨ ij
  Ft. Mist. \

  ℞
   Spirit Formic. ℥ij
   Liq. Anodyn. Hofm.
   Bals. vit. Hofm āā ℥ss
   Aqua Menth. pip.
   ——Serpyll āā ℥ jj
  Ft. Lotio.

He took it away with him, and promised to let
me know the result. In a few weeks afterwards
he called upon me again, and declared himself
quite satisfied that my remedies could not be
obtained in England, as he had sent the prescription to several of the first druggists in London,
and none of them appeared to have even heard of
the drugs therein prescribed, and also informed
me, which was more satisfactory for me to hear,
that he was progressing towards recovery.

Another instance may be given. The following is a very excellent diet drink, which I have found most beneficial in my practice: all the principal ingredients, however, are articles which cannot be obtained in this country:

R

Flor. Siccat. Lamii.
Rad. Cyeri.
Rad. Galang.
Bistori.
Osmund. regal.
Flor. ras. rubr.
Ichthyocoll.

Now, these examples are a good as a hundred. The first ingredient in the lotion is a spirit made from ants, and is one of the most effectual remedies, applied externally to the generative organs, that is known in any part of the world, and yet no one in England uses it but myself.

In fact the British Pharmacopœia is exceedingly limited in remedies of this kind; and no man can treat these cases successfully, who has not other medicines than that contained in it.

The treatment must, of course, vary very materially, accordingly as the symptoms, constitution or other circumstances may indicate.

In that class of cases in which there are frequent nocturnal emissions, accompanied by no positive evidence that the disease has as yet affected the general system, I have found an occasional warm hip-bath, taken on going to bed, with internal administration of Elixir roborans Whytii, and Extract of Centaur. minoris, to be beneficial.

In another class of patients, in which the symptoms are of a lower type, erections feeble, emissions easily provoked, the habit of masturbation either practised or having been practised. I find cold-water applications externally combined with internal administration of Bromuret of Potass. Balsam Vitæ Hoffmani, and Aq. Carminatio Regia, of much utility; while in other cases, again, I give Extracts of Trifalium fibrini, Satureja, Serpentaria, &c.

In some cases of impotence I have administered with very great effect a lozenge (Morsuli), prepared according to the following formula:

℞

Bolet. Cervin.	Semin. Eruc. Fraxia.
Priap. Cerv.	Borac. Venet.
Stin. Marin.	Piper Alb.
Radic Pyret.	Cardam.
Rad. Satyrii Eryng.	Spec. imper.
Nuc. Indic.	Vaniglæ.

Sachar. alb. in Aqua Cinam. Solv. Minut. incisa et pulveris misceantur a fiąt l. a. Morsuļi. Si completi desiderantur, adde Ambergis Moschi. Tibet.

The proportional quantity of the ingredients mentioned, and the number and frequency of the morsuli to be taken, will depend, of course, on the peculiarities of the case, &c. I may mention that most of the foregoing remedies, and others mentioned in other parts of the work as being employed by me, are only to be found in foreign Pharmacopœias.

From Chapter VII., "Remarks on False Delicacy," I quote the following:—

One of the most remarkable and melancholy facts, perhaps, which the history of medical science discloses, is that the most important branch of it, viz., sexual physiology, has been studiously ignored. It may safely be affirmed that nearly two-thirds of the "ills that flesh is heir to," are traceable to abuses of the generative organism, and that at least one-half of those abuses are attributable to general ignorance as to the nature and functions of that organism. But not only are the sufferers themselves ignorant, but those who should have been able to instruct and relieve them are scarcely less devoid of the knowledge essential for that purpose.

It is satisfactory to know that there are a few men of eminence who do not suffer themselves to be influenced by such absurd and prejudicial ideas.

In one of his celebrated Physiological Lectures Dr. Lawrence observes in reference to the fatal effects of *ignoring* or *misunderstanding* the consequences of abuses of the generative organism: —"I have had occasion frequently to observe that medical skill has failed in what were represented and appeared to be cases commonly called decline, simply because *one important feature of the case* has been concealed from the physician, and *because he had failed to enquire as to its existence*; I mean the decay of those portions and functions of the human frame which delicacy veils most scrupulously from the human eye, and affections of which seem, by some great mistake, to have been placed without the pale to which ordinary practice confines itself."

These just and sensible remarks bring me to the main object which I had in introducing the subject of the false delicacy to which I have thus been adverting, viz., to impress upon the reader that there is no more real necessity for avoiding the consultation of the enlightened medical practitioner, or when consulted, for withholding from him the slightest fact which may concern the preservation or restoration of our health, than there is for avoiding the consultation of a solicitor when our property is endangered, or keeping from his knowledge facts which would enable him to preserve or recover it. Yet we readily give the fullest possible information unreservedly to the latter, and either altogether withhold, or delay it until too late for the former. This cannot arise from mere want of confidence, as it is proverbial that good faith and absolute secrecy characterise equally the sacred confidences of solicitor and client, and physician and patient.

The reason why so many hundreds spend a life of misery, or sink to an early grave, when a timely and simple treatment would have restored happiness and health, is that feeling of false delicacy which it is impossible to condemn in terms sufficiently strong.

Innumerable instances have occurred within my practice, of patients who have consulted me a considerable time after reading one of my Essays, and on my expressing surprise that they had delayed so long, the reply has usually been twofold—firstly, the matter was such a "delicate" one that they could not bear to speak of it to a stranger; secondly, that they fancied I might look upon their follies with such disgust and contempt as would prevent me from efficiently relieving them. I need scarcely say that in the first case they are sacrificing their health to an "idea," and in the second they are of course utterly mistaken. I adduce these instances, because they may be and are hundreds of others who entertain and act upon similar ideas.

SELF DIAGNOSIS;

OR,

"HOW SHALL WE ASCERTAIN UNDER WHAT AF-FECTION WE ARE SUFFERING?"

[This Chapter (Chapter IX.) is inserted in full]

In consequence of the frequent inquires made of me, "How shall I *know* whether I am suffering from spermatorrhœa? What are the symptoms by which I shall be able to recognise it, or by which it will be accompanied?" I am induced to add a few words on this important point.

The symptoms are infinitely varied, extremely numerous, and differ greatly in different cases, both in number, nature and degree. It will be well, perhaps, first to put the most prominent of them into a tabular form, and then to introduce one or two illustrative cases.

To render this tabulation more intelligible, the symptoms are divided into LOCAL, *i.e.*, affections of the generative organs; BODILY, *i. e.*, affections of the muscular, circulative, nutritive, and respiratory systems; and MENTAL, *i. e.*, affections of the nervous system.

In the first place, as being not only most definite in character, but also as indicative of the disease being more than usually deeply seated

and confirmed, the local symptoms may be
mentioned. They are as follows:—

Local Symptoms.

Pollutions* accompanying expulsion of urine.
Pollutions accompanying defæcation.
Erections and emissions upon slight excitement, such
  as the mere presence of females, or juxtaposition
  of their dress, &c.
Emissions under similar circumstances, unaccom-
  panied by erection.
Nocturnal pollutions, with or without erection or
  consciousness.
Diurnal pollutions.
Spermatic urine.
Contraction of the foreskin.
Spasmodic or dull pains occasionally in the organs.
Varicocele, or varicose veins in the testicles.
Pimples on shoulders and forehead.
Premature emission during coitus.
Priapism, or erections apparently without any ex-
  citing cause.
Decrease of sexual desire or enjoyment.
Sanguineous emission.
Diminution in size of the penis and other organs.
Want or imperfection of erectile power.
Climax—Impotence.

In reference to *general symptoms* it is necessary
to observe that many, if not all, of these symptoms
may occur in and denote forms of ordinary
disease; but if produced by spermatorrhœa, they
will be aggravated in degree, and will not yield
to treatment known to be eradicative of them in
ordinary cases. This fact could be illustrated in
a variety of instances, but one may suffice. In an

* The terms "pollutions" and "emissions" refer
to involuntary escapes of seminal fluid.

otherwise healthy person an attack of indigestion,
originating in inattention to diet, will yield to
gentle purgatives, tonics, and other well-known
means; but if the symptoms of indigestion exist
in consequence of the impairment of the nutritive
functions by seminal losses, the ordinary remedies
for such symptoms fail to produce their usual
effect, as until the *primary* cause of the symptoms
be removed, the effect will not only continue, but
increase. In like manner, disorders in respiration
and circulation may arise indifferently from spermatorrhœa, or from other causes; in the latter
case the remedies usually indicated for such
symptoms will remove them, but not so if they
be caused by spermatorrhœa; and it may be
mentioned that it has been clearly ascertained,
that there is no single function of the animal
economy but may not become deranged by long
continued involuntary seminal losses.

GENERAL SYMPTOMS—BODILY.

Muscular, Respiratory, Circulative, and Nutritive Systems.

Increased appetite or voracity (in early stages).
Gnawing, and heat of epigastrium.
Uneasiness, sinking or faintness before taking food
    followed by disgust or nausea afterwards.
Want of appetite for plain kinds of food.
Weight in epigastrium.
Quickened pulse.
Flushed face.
Acid eructations.
Acrid heat at the upper part of œsophagus.
Alteration in secretions of liver and pancreas.
Evolution of flatus.
Colic.
Griping.

Difficulty of Breathing and Cough.
Distention of stomach and intestines.
Muscular flaccidity.
Excessive mucous secretions.
Irregular action of the heart.
Apoplexy.
Liquid and unnatural stools.
Diarrhœa.
Inflammation of rectum.
Constipation.
Loss of substance.
Cadaverous appearance of skin.
Hollow or sunken eyes.
Extreme sensibility to cold.
Rheumatism.
Loss of Hair.
Pulmonary Catarrh.
Indolence, or indisposition to exercise.
Lassitude.
Fatigue on slight exertion.

CLIMAX—CONFIRMED DEBILITY.

GENERAL SYMPTOMS—MENTAL.

Nervous System.

Restlessness.
Sighing.
Sensation of congestion
Want of energy.
Uncertainty of tone of voice.
Nervous asthma.
Vertigo.
Want of purpose.
Dimness of sight.
Weakness of hearing.
Aversion to society.
Blushing.
Want of confidence.
Avoidance of conversation.

Desire for solitude.
Listlessness and inability to fix the attention.
Cowardice.
Depression of spirits.
Giddiness
Loss of memory.
Excitability of temper.
Moroseness.
Want of fixity of attention.
Disposition to ruminate.
Trembling of the hands.
Sudden pallor.
Lachrymosity.
Tremor from slight causes.
Pains in back of the head or the spine.
Pains over the eyes.
Disturbed and unrefreshing sleep.
Strange and lascivious dreams.
Hypochondriasis.
CLIMAX—INSANITY.

The following additional illustrative cases are
by no means selected because they present features
of great severity, but because they are specimens
of the most ordinary cases upon which I am
consulted; and save that every expression which
could afford the slightest clue to the individu-
ality of the patients themselves has been carefully
eliminated, they are the verbatim statements of
the patients themselves. In order to avoid un-
necessary repetition, it may be mentioned that
every one of the following cases, and many thousands of similar, and even far more serious ones,
have been *successfully treated* by me during the
twenty years over which my practice has extended.

CASE No. 874.

I have been in the filthy habit of practising self-pollution from about the age of 14, when at school, until I was 24. I then married, which is now about a year and a half ago, but am ashamed to say, that so completely had the habit taken hold of me that I have even (though not often, practised it since that time, till lately, in fact, when I procured a copy of your "Philosophy of Marriage." I must mention that I am naturally of a good constitution, but for nearly twelve months past I have gradually been getting thinner and thinner, as though I was wasting away. I appear to be in excellent health, but am very speedily tired with the slightest exertion; my appetite is poor, I have no energy, am extremely nervous, and frequently overcome by melancholy; my memory is becoming defective, and I have a very tiresome little cough, with a sort of choking sensation when attempting to read aloud, especially after a meal; the left testicle hangs a little lower than the right one, and after the urine has been allowed to stand for a time a white cloudy secretion appears to be floating about in it, and a sort of greasy looking scum forms on top. I am also troubled by frequent emissions during sleep all which symptoms induce me to think I must be suffering from Spermatorrhœa, and trust you will be able to do something to relieve me. I applied to a medical man, who is esteemed very clever in this neighbourhood, but he said he could not see any complaint, save my getting thin, for which he advised change of air, and gave me quinine, but no good effects have followed.

___

The treatment thus referred to was unsuccessful, because it did not touch the deep-seated cause of the symptoms.

___

CASE No. 2116.

I can no longer conceal from myself that I am suffering from Spermatorrhœa, the result of that wicked habit contracted even before I was in my teens; I even forget how, and how early it was contracted, and although I have sometimes abandoned it for a time I have always relapsed again into it, and have only lately been able to feel that I have at length mastered it. My age is now 26, and although having been three years at the sea side, every one congratulates me upon my health and appearance, I am quite conscious of the unreality of those appearances. My nerves are seriously impaired, I have very frequent nocturnal emissions; the spirit I once possessed I am afraid is for ever gone, and the sense of fatigue I experience on undertaking the smallest labor, and the flaccid feel of the muscles, renders me doubtful of the possibility of their effective reparation; I cannot fix my attention on my business, make sad blunders, and get very excitable and ill-tempered. For the last few months, too, I have experienced a dull pain or uneasiness in the testicles, especially on the left

side, and have occasional darting pains of a
spasmodic character in the penis, as though
they suddenly received a most severe and acute
electric shock.

In this case, although there were well marked
local symptoms, the mischief had principally
developed itself in the impairment of the nervous system.

CASE No. 1375.

It is with great reluctance I pen the following
letter:—

I began to indulge in masturbation or Onanism
some years ago; I do not exactly know how long
since. It was brought about by accident. Since
your work on marriage fell into my hands, I have
resisted the temptation to defile myself. At first
it was very difficult; and I could scarcely restrain
myself for a week. I have now managed to do so
for about three weeks, but feel tortured with all
sorts of vicious thoughts. This is my situation
at present, but previously, and for some years,
scarcely a day passed over in which I did not
practise self-pollution. I am considerably troubled
with knots of tough mucous matter coming up
my throat; this always occurred two or three
hours after masturbation. As it has very considerably decreased lately, I now attribute the
symptoms to that cause, which I did not previously
suspect. My urine is sometimes very muddy, a sort

of glyt is found to stick against the side of the
urinal, and small white specks are sometimes ob-
servable floating about in the urine. I have a
tendency to be costive, but not specially so, I have
not the power of erection I ought to have. I begin
to feel weak, and not able to work as I used to
do ; and when I rise in the morning I do not feel
refreshed after my night's sleep. I have occasionally a throbbing pain at the end of the foreskin,
which is swelled, and appears somewhat inflamed,
and I am very subject to pleasure dreams, which
are very weakening. I have slight aching pains
in the testicles, one of which is slightly wasted,
and have pains across the loins and up the neck
and back of the head, which I never had before.

CASE No. 1146.

I feel myself constrained to fly to you at last,
and reveal a secret which I can no longer keep
to myself. You will readily understand what it
is, and I am filled with shame to acknowledge it,
but have been doing it in ignorance until the last
year or two. I am one of those unhappy beings
who early fell a victim to that accursed habit—
masturbation, or self-pollution, when at school. I
will describe all the particulars. I am now twenty-
five years of age ; it was when I was about fourteen I commenced that self-abuse, and sometimes
I had sexual intercourse. About four years ago
I had the disease called gonorrhœa, or clap, my
doctor called it. He cured me, as I thought, but

I still kept practising that pernicious habit. About two years ago, or nearly, I felt a tremendous prickly itching underneath the testicles, so I went to my doctor again, and he told me it was gleet. I have been taking lots of stuff and injections, but they don't do me any good. There is scarcely any pain, but an almost continual discharge, which causes a stain like gum to be left on my linen. It is much aggravated by taking wine or spirits, or violent exercise; it affects my eyes very considerably. I only wish I had read your book before, for I had made up my mind previously to reading it that I should never be cured. My habits are pretty regular, and my occupation out-door. I feel a loss of memory and a continued feeling of languidness, being tired with the least exertion, very nervous and timid; the eyes are very weak and sometimes very hot, and feel sore in their sockets. I have pains also in the back of my head; my sleep don't afford me much refreshment, for I very often feel more tired and languid when I get up than when I go to bed. I am troubled with dreams, and sometimes fancy myself in the embrace of some beautiful woman; and on some of these occasions I have my night clothes wet with the fluid which has escaped. The last one occurred only two nights ago: and for the last two years I have had escape of seminal fluid when in company of females. My water is generally of a high colour. I am very low spirited, although I used to be full of life.

CASE No. 1735.

I am suffering from the effects of self-abuse, practised until recently. I am now twenty-three years of age, tall and thin. When in company of females the penis is continually wet with thin semen, sometimes with erection, sometimes without. I have never had connection with any female, and if I did, the emission would come far too soon. My forehead and shoulders are covered with pimples, the former being very much disfigured, and they are always worse after an emission in the night, which occurs without erection. My eyes are bloodshot at times, and water in a breeze of wind, particularly in the morning. The testicles hang very low, the left is varicose, and there are no wrinkles at all in the scrotum on that side. The dribbling, when in company of women, is very odd and unpleasant. When my urine has stood a few hours, there is generally a sediment. Is there any fear of the right testicle becoming varicose also from hanging?

CASE No. 865.

I am twenty-seven years of age, of a delicate, nervous temperament; I am single, and likely to remain so, unless you can assist me; for there is no disguising the fact, I am *impotent* through the effects of self-pollution, which I practised from eleven years of age until twenty-two, when I became acquainted with its mischief and left it off

for ever. I then obtained medical advice, which
gave me only temporary relief, and I have since
applied to another medical man, who gave me
tonics, but I am grieved to say without effect.
My bowels are regular, as I am very careful in
my diet; I am much afraid I am suffering from
spermatorrhœa, as I have noticed that the last
drop of urine is thick and ropy, and there is
always a copious discharge of semen after any
excitement by being in female society, and I have
very frequent nocturnal emissions. The testicles
and penis are very small, and there is something
like a lot of hard cords attached to the left testicle.
I have a slight cough always on me, with short-
ness of breathing, and I am very thin. I often
turn very giddy when rising or stooping hurriedly.
Reading the slightest thing of a sentimental
character brings tears to my eyes, which I cannot
help, although I feel them to be maudlin. My
sight is weak. I have no confidence in myself.
I blush and look guilty at the slightest thing
said to me, whether right or wrong; blushing
and becoming pallid by turns. I find my constitution is weakened most terribly. I have got
very thin this last month, and have had nocturnal emissions sometimes two or three nights
running. Sometimes, on going to stool, a thick
gummy matter comes from the penis, and there
is a slight irritation at the root of the penis, after
passing it. I have slight pains in the back, and
sometimes in the testicles.

CASE No. 682.

At the age of fourteen or fifteen I was taught the disgraceful habit of self-pollution by a companion, and continued to practice it until twenty, when a friend, who knew something of anatomy, &c., told me the consequences, and caused me to leave it off in disgust. I am, however, troubled with frequent emissions, accompanied with disturbing dreams. I have sometimes put some of my urine in a bottle, when I have noticed, after a few hours, a filmy substance floating about in it, and when it has stood a week, it has become quite thick at the bottom. My testicles are very pendulous, and I sometimes feel a slight escape of semen when in the company of females. My left testicle is smaller than the right, and has more cords or veins about it. The white of my eyes is generally of a muddy or brownish colour, and my sight is certainly not so good as it was formerly. I have also been troubled with pimples about my face and shoulders, which are very disagreeable. I am troubled with extreme nervousness, involuntary blushings, weakness of sight, lassitude, coldness of the extremities, and sometimes pains in the head and loins. I get rheumatism by the very slightest draught, sometimes within a quarter of an hour after exposure to it, and occasionally it is a long time before I can get rid of it, and it is frequently severe.

Case No. 2371.

From 12 to 18 I practised the habit of masturbation almost continuously, having learnt it from my schoolfellows, and neither I nor any of my companions ever for a moment suspected that we were injuring ourselves in any way. A fearful mistake as I now know to my cost. I left it off because I thought it a filthy habit, and since have occasionally had sexual intercourse. On some of these occasions I have been able to have full and proper connexion, at another time there is premature emission, and sometimes I fail altogether to have an erection, and seminal fluid will pass without any sensation. Occasionally, too, a dull pain follows near the root of the penis, a most uneasy sensation. There is never any certainty in my attempts at coition. I am frequently troubled with lascivious dreams, and sometimes with others of a less agreeable kind, but always causing me to rise without benefit from my rest. All these things were a mystery to me until I read your book, which completely opened my eyes to the real state of the case. My appetite is very bad; I am altogether unwell, fearfully languid all day long, I always go to bed tired, and with an aching pain in my legs, and rise in the morning the same, never feeling better for rest. My face sometimes breaks out in spots, and I look thin and ill. In fact I *feel* ill; I am afraid I have destroyed all generative power, especially as for some time past I have not only been afraid

to contemplate intercourse from the fear of fail-
ure, but when opportunity has offered, have
really experienced a total want of desire.

———

In many instances where circumstances compel
the treatment to be by correspondence only, I find
that the injury to the nervous system of the
patients is such, that, after forwarding a full detail of their case, I shall perhaps have a letter by
the next post to tell me that they have overrated
the symptoms, and that they feel quite well and
fancy they have been nervous almost without a
cause, and a post or two after will bring a letter
that they are thoroughly wretched and despondent
They are troubled by miserable fancies that their
letters are opened and read by unknown parties
before coming to hand : that everyone who meets
them sees in their countenance the effects of their
habits, or is aware in some mysterious way of their
ill-practices. Others tell me that the blood rushes
to their face whenever a casual eye meets them
in the street, frequently accompanied by perspiration, and that the eyes are involuntary cast
down, as though they had been suddenly detected
in some guilty act : that their conversation becomes disconnected and their observation desul-
tory : that they lose all their relish for pursuits
which formerly interested them to the highest
degree : that they envy every one they see, fancy
that there is nothing left for them in the world,
either of utility or pleasure ; that they have be-

come aimless and purposeless, and that all they can do is to drag on a miserable existence till the tomb closes over them.

Although spermatorrhœa and its host of accompanying evils in the majority of cases, caused by practices of the kind spoken of in the preceding cases, it is not invariably the case that it is so. Spermatorrhœa may be caused by constipation, by ascarides, or worms in the rectum, by stricture of the rectum, and many other circumstances, some of these are easy of removal, others more difficult; but in all such cases the removal of the cause is immediately followed by the disappearance of the spermatorrhœa.

The foregoing extracts are but a small part of the whole book, and will doubtless be found *comparatively* obscure on account of the absence of the context. Those who would further acquaint themselves with the subject, and are anxious to become cognizant with every particular connected with the structure, functions and derangements of the generative organs, may do so by procuring a copy of the work itself.

APPENDIX.

THE work from which the preceding extracts are taken has now reached its Forty-seventh Edition (of five thousand copies each) and has been read by all classes of society, from the highest to the lowest. It affords me great gratification that not only has the work itself been thus extensively circulated, but that it has elicited from persons of the highest intelligence and education, the most unqualified expressions of approval.

During the time these sheets were passing through the press I received the following :—

" Montrose, N.B.,
September 23rd., 1861.
" Dear Sir,
"I have read with great pleasure and profit your work 'The Philosophy of Marriage.' It is a great pity that such a work is not more universally known, as much evil and suffering might be prevented. But there are so many trashy effusions in print on the subject, that I believe many are afraid to get or read any work on the subject at all, supposing all to be alike.

"May the time soon come when the *false* delicacy, which is allowing sin so much to prevail among us, shall give place to a far *sounder* and DEEPER ONE, based on knowledge of the truths of nature and the purity of Christian principles. In every human heart there is implanted an intense desire for knowledge, especially in such matters, and while this false delicacy enshrouds the subject in mystery, which only increases the desire for knowing, need we wonder that much sin is often committed in this search, and often through sheer igno. rance? O that parents and guardians would only rightly learn, think, and teach!

"I am, yours truly,

"PETER GIBB,

"Dr. Kahn."   "N.E.C. Missionary."

The cogency of the sentiments expressed in the latter part of the foregoing letter, and the earnest and forcible manner in which they are enunciated, made me naturally desirous of introducing them in my subsequent publications, and in reply to my letter soliciting the requisite permission of the writer, that gentleman replies (*inter alia*) as follows:—

"Montrose, September 27th, 1861.

"Dear Sir,—

  "I have a feeling of repugnance somehow to my name appearing in print. And yet I feel that if I can do any good, I have no right to withhold it. . . . But if you are satisfied that the cause of truth and humanity can be served more by publishing my letter with my name than by any other means at your command, I will give you full permission, and leave the consequences with my God.

" Perhaps you will allow me to make a few suggestions which I think might be profitably acted on in any future editions of the book (or which might, in the form of a fly-leaf, accompany the present one.) I think you would do well to insert a few sentences on the *moral, social, and religious, as well as physical evils* resulting from *any use* of the generative functions, except in the marriage state. Your book will, doubtless, fall into the hands of many who disregard or avoid any homily on the subject from ministers or others; but who could not get past it when thus forced on them in such a work.

" Illegitimacy has arisen with us, at least in some parts of Scotland, to the rank of a terrible social evil, and if you would unmistakeably raise your voice in *thunder tones* against it, you might render a great service to society, and you would much more fully enlist the sympathies of these who view it in a moral or religious aspect alone; and who look with suspicion on all who reveal any of the secrets of nature, regarding such as tending to inflame the passions—and this it may, in some depraved cases do. But by your adopting the course I have hinted at, I think you might effectually place youself and book on the other side, and in such a case I could most willingly give you my name.

" I am, yours truly,

" Dr. Kahn."   " PETER GIBB."

These valuable remarks I most fully and thoroughly endorse, and I do not think I could possibly express them in more forcible language. Of the frightful *physical* results arising from the use of the generative functions when unsanctioned by the marriage tie, one of the departments of my Museum affords ample indication; but they are not for a moment to be compared with the injuries inflicted on society, *socially* and *morally* —injuries which it is impossible to over-estimate; and, in giving publicity to such comments as those of Mr. Gibb, I feel that I am promoting the cause of public virtue and morality.

L. J. KAHN, M.D.

☞ I may remark, previously to introducing the following Instructions, that many are deterred from applying for professional aid in consequence of the supposition that their cases are beyond cure. I wish it therefore to be understood that during the whole period of my practice in this country, now eleven years, I have never met with one so severe as to baffle me, and that I have been called upon to treat, and have treated successfully, cases, far more difficult than any I have met with in my practice abroad.

THE FOLLOWING INSTRUCTIONS

Are given for the purpose of facilitating Invalids in obtaining Dr. KAHN'S advice.

His hours of consultation are from 11 a.m. to 8 p.m. at the Consulting Rooms attached to his Museum, top of the Haymarket.

Patients who desire to be treated by correspondence should observe the following instructions :—

1.—Their letters should contain full particulars as to age—Constitution or temperament—Habits as to occupation—Mode of living—Whether married or single—Supposed cause of affection—Condition of bowels—Ordinary state of urine—State of particular organs affected, and—Whether any, and if so, what treatment has been previously adopted.

2.—The letters may, at the option of the patient, be either signed with his own name or an assumed one or initials, as circumstances may render expedient, and must contain a remittance of Dr. Kahn's Consultation Fee of One Guinea.

INTRODUCTIONS.

3—The replies will be addressed, either direct or to post-office till called for, or in any other-manner desired ; but in every case the address to which they are to be forwarded should be clearly indicated, and fully and legibly written.

4—In small towns or villages, where there may be an objection on the part of the patient to the name of Dr. KAHN being seen on a letter addressed to him, he may direct to L. J. K., 8, Tichborne Street, Haymarket, London, W.

5—The remedies can be forwarded to *all parts of the world*, carefully packed and screened from observation, and will be addressed strictly according to the instructions of the patient, which instructions should *be clear and unmistakeable*.

6—Dr. KAHN wishes to impress upon all patients *with whom it is at all practicable*, the importance of affording him at least one personal interview, as the advantages resulting to them from such a course will, by the increased certainty and celerity of the treatment, more than repay them the trouble and expense thereby occasioned. Should this, however, be impracticable or inconvenient, the patient should procure a small stoppered Bottle, enclosed within a turned boxwood case (which may be procured at any respectable Chemist's or Perfumer's), and forward therein the last few drops of urine voided on rising in the morning.—A bottle thus protected, may be sent by post; but, should any difficulty be experienced in obtaining such a bottle and case, the urine may be sent in an ordinary phial carefully packed, but in this case it must be forwarded by rail.

N.B.—All communications to L. J. KAHN, whether by name or initials, should be addressed to 3, Tichborne Street, Haymarket, London, W.

NOTICE.

In consequence of the great demands made upon Dr. L. J. KAHN'S time, by his practice at his Museum, he cannot longer be consulted at his Private Residence. He will therefore, be in attendance at the Consulting Rooms attached to the Museum, 8, Tichborne Street, (top of the Haymarket), DAILY from 11 a.m. to 8 p.m.

All Letters and Communications must be addressed to 3, Tichborne Street, Haymarket, London, W.

www.ingramcontent.com/pod-product-compliance
Lightning Source LLC
Chambersburg PA
CBHW030604270326
41927CB00007B/1038